"Unseen Footsteps of Jesus"

OLAM HABA

(Future World)

Mysteries Book 5-"Storm Clouds"

Jerry Ayers

authorHOUSE

AuthorHouse™
1663 Liberty Drive
Bloomington, IN 47403
www.authorhouse.com
Phone: 833-262-8899

© *2023 Jerry Ayers. All rights reserved.*

No part of this book may be reproduced, stored in a retrieval system, or transmitted by any means without the written permission of the author.

Published by AuthorHouse 02/03/2023

ISBN: 978-1-7283-7801-5 (sc)
ISBN: 978-1-7283-7799-5 (hc)
ISBN: 978-1-7283-7800-8 (e)

Library of Congress Control Number: 2023901778

Print information available on the last page.

Any people depicted in stock imagery provided by Getty Images are models, and such images are being used for illustrative purposes only.
Certain stock imagery © Getty Images.

This book is printed on acid-free paper.

Because of the dynamic nature of the Internet, any web addresses or links contained in this book may have changed since publication and may no longer be valid. The views expressed in this work are solely those of the author and do not necessarily reflect the views of the publisher, and the publisher hereby disclaims any responsibility for them.

CONTENTS

Chapter 1 1
Chapter 2 13
Chapter 3 27
Chapter 4 37
Chapter 5 49
Chapter 6 62
Chapter 7 71
Chapter 8 84
Chapter 9 95
Chapter 10 106
Chapter 11 113
Chapter 12 128

I...the cunning serpent began to raise its head off the grassy floor of the garden when Yahusha quickly stomped on its head with His heel killing the demonic minion of Satan instantly. This verified the prediction in the Holy Writ Scripture in the book of *Bre'shiyth* (Genesis) chapter three and verse fourteen, ***"Yahuah Yah said to the hissing snake, 'Because you have done this, you are cursed because you are evil more than any other four-legged animal and more than any other living thing in the spread out field. On your belly you will crawl and eat dust all the days of your life. Hatred I will place between you and the woman, between your seed and her Seed. He will open your head wide like a mouth and you will snap at His heel."*** Then Yahusha commanded the evil spirit Deception which had possessed the creature to be sentenced to an arid, dry place for punishment until the Messianic Period. The other part of the spirit called Death had departed instantly from the slithering sickly yellowish-green creature upon it finishing life and had fled to Hades under the protection of the dark lord Satan.

Then Yahusha came to Kepha (Peter), Ya'kov (James) and his brother Yowchanan (John) a third time and said to them, "Lie down and rest and fall asleep for what remains and be refreshed. It is sufficient now. Look, soon the hour approaches near and the Son of Man will be yielded up into the hands of sinners!" A little more than an hour later, Yahusha commanded the Chosen Eleven, "Rise and awaken from your sleep. Let us go. Look now, the one yielding Me up is approaching near!" Then Yahusha and the Eleven began to leave their spot in the garden back across the Brook of *Qidrown* (Kidron), a storm torrent near the Great City Yruwshalaim (Jerusalem). While He was talking to the Chosen Eleven, Yhuwdah (Judah) one of the Twelve came and with him was a great throng of rabble with lanterns, lamps, knives and wooden clubs from the high priests and senior members of the Sanhedrin of the people. Yhuwdah (Judah/Judas) who was yielding Him up gave to the crowd a mutual and preplanned indication stating, "Whomever I embrace to kiss, it is He. Use strength and seize and retain Him to securely take Him off!" So, at once approaching and coming near to Yahusha he said, "Be well, *Rhabbi* (Teacher) my Master!" Then he earnestly kissed Him on the cheek. Yahusha responded, "Comrade, why are you near at hand? Do you yield up the Son of Man with a kiss?" Those around Him saw what was about to happen and asked the Messiah, "Master, should we strike with our war knives?"

Then Yahusha asked the crowd, "Whom do you seek?" They said, "Yahusha of Nazareth!" So, He responded, "I EXIST." When the Messiah said 'I Exist' they all backed off and fell to the ground. Once more Yahusha inquired of the crowd, "Whom do you seek?" They responded, "Yahusha of Nazareth!" Yahusha then said, "I said to you that I EXIST. Certainly, if you seek Me allow the rest of these to withdraw." Then approaching quickly were the guards from the Temple and they threw with force their hand on Yahusha and used strength to seize Him. Then Shim'own Kepha (Simon Peter) standing next to Yahusha extended his hand and unsheathed his knife and with a single blow like the sting of a scorpion knocked with the weapon the side of the head of the slave of the chief priest and removed by amputation his right ear. The name of that slave was *Melek* (Malchus). Yahusha commanded, "Put back your knife to its location! For this reason, all those taking the war knife will be destroyed fully and perish by the war knife. Or do you not know that I am able just now to invoke My Father and He would stand beside Me more than twelve legions of angels (seventy-two thousand)! How then would the Holy Writ of the Scriptures be verified and come into being?" Then Yahusha turned to the slave of the high priest and said to him, "Allow this." Next without picking up the ear from the ground He touched the salves right ear and He cured him by restoring his severed ear like it was before.

Then in that hour Yahusha turned to the throng of rabble and inquired, "In this manner did you issue forth upon a plundering brigand with war knives and wooden clubs to seize and capture Me for arrest? I sat down with you daily teaching in the Temple and you did not use strength to seize and retain Me. But this all had to come into being in order that the Holy Writ of the Scriptures may verify the predictions of the inspired prophets. This is your hour and your master is that of obscure shadiness!" Then His Chosen Eleven all issued forth and vanished by running away. Also, one of the young pupils, a youth under forty years old had thrown all around his nude body a bleached linen cloth and the guards used strength to seize him too. However, he abandoned and left behind the bleached linen cloth escaping and ran away from them completely nude.

Then the temple guards seized the arms of Yahusha with extreme force and began to beat Him in the face and mid-section bruising His face and ribs. After they had beat Him down they looped a very ruff rope around His throat until they shackled His hands and feet with iron clasps and chain. Once the chains were tightly secured, they yanked on the chains making the Messiah lunge forward as if leading a rabid dog to be caged. Their destination was to take Him to stand in front of *HaGadowl Kohen* (the chief priest) Kaiaphas. During the long walk the temple guards would beat the Messiah over the head or strike His body with the end of the chains continuing to bruise His already battered body leaving additional black and blue marks and swelling from the malicious hammerings of the temple guards as they mocked Him. The crowd following the temple guards shouted obscenities and encouraged the random beatings by the *Yhuwdiy* (Jewish) temple guards.

While the Messiah was being rounded up and shackled like a rabid and dangerous animal, other temple guards were sent out by order of Kaiaphas to selected scribes and senior members of the Sanhedrin to convene a meeting at his house at this very late hour. They were not told that it was going to be a trial because a trial after sundown is strictly forbidden by the Law of the Hebrews. The guards were also instructed to pay by bribe from the temple treasury drunks, the homeless living on the streets or in dark corners and even derelicts of society to fill the meeting room of the home of Kaiaphas. The Roman horse night patrol began to watch this very unusual activity in the Upper City of Yruwshalaim (Jerusalem). The temple guards would wave or nod their heads towards the mounted Roman soldiers as if everything was ok, yet it just did not feel right to the horsemen. Finally, one of the mounted Roman patrol asked one of the *Yhuwdiy* (Jewish) temple guards, "*Quis est venio?*" (What is happening?) The temple guard smiled, shrugged his shoulders and responded, "*Kibelah ash'pah h'alats reh'khov!*" (Getting the garbage off the streets). However, the Roman patrol continued to keep watch.

Before Yahusha was taken to Kaiaphas, He was led to the house of *Chananyah ben Seth* (Ananus son of Seth) the retired *Gadowl Kohen* (chief priest) because he was the father of the wife of Kaiaphas and wielded the ultimate political and social power of the ruling priesthood. *Chananyah* (Ananus) was awake and waiting upon the arrival of the temple guards because he was the first to be informed of the arrest of Yahusha. Kepha (Peter) and Yowchanan (John) followed the temple guards and the Messiah at a great distance so as not to be seen. The Messiah was violently stood in front of *Chananyah* who began clucking his tongue and shaking his head. He looked Yahusha over from head to toe. The once pure white tunic of Yahusha was now soiled and stained with blood from being beaten down to the ground and kicked with the soiled sandals of the temple guards. His curly black hair was in array from the repeated pummeling and a half-dried stream of blood was present from the corner of His mouth and ran down into the beard on His chin. His face was partially swollen and under His eyes was black and blue where He had been beaten with the fists of the temple guards. Then *Chananyah* (Ananus) hissed, "So this is the criminal that has been causing such trouble and grief amongst our brothers!" Then he spat in the face of the Messiah. As the spittle ran down the face of Yahusha, *Chananyah* continued, "You call yourself a *navi* (prophet)? You are nothing but a *busha ve-kherpa* (total disgrace)! *Kakh kelev chathan sheli* (take this dog to my son-in-law)!" Then the temple guards viciously yanked on the chains that were bound to the feet and hands of Yahusha and led Him from out of the presence of *Chananyah ben Seth* (Ananus son of Seth).

The temple guards led Him through the narrow streets of the Upper City. They jabbed the Messiah in the ribs with the blunt end of their spears if they felt He was not walking fast enough or would smack Him with the wooden handle of their long lances for pure enjoyment. The atmosphere of the night had changed. The heavy fog had now blanked the entire Great City of Yruwshalaim (Jerusalem) the thick white envelope made the torches work overtime and the late night air had become very chilly. When they arrived at the outer gates of the residence of Kaiaphas, one of the women followers of Yahusha ran up to the mounted Roman patrol and exclaimed,

"Stop them they have arrested an innocent man!" Immediately one of the temple guards seized her by the shoulders and forced her back towards the gates of the courtyard. He held both arms up and shrugged his shoulders and said to the mounted patrol, *"Meh'sho'ga!"* (crazy) with a big grin as she was ushered inside the gates by another temple guard. Then one of the mounted Roman soldiers said to the other horseman, *"Gradi propono dux Cornelius tumultus exorsus!* (Go tell Commander Cornelius a riot has begun!) The second horseman hesitated and the first one yelled, *"Gradi! Gradi!* (Go! Go!) The second horseman reigned his horse around and took off up the cobblestone streets making a rapid clop-clop-clop sound as the horse trotted away.

Kepha and Yowchanan followed Yahusha and the temple guards from the house of *Chananyah ben Seth* (Ananus son of Seth) the retired *Gadowl Kohen* (chief priest) to the mansion of Kaiaphas. However, they had got separated in the crowd and Yowchanan (John) arrived first and since he was known by the family of Kaiaphas he entered into the gate of the yard open to the wind of the mansion in the company of Yahusha. Realizing that Kepha (Peter) was not in the open courtyard, Yowchanan went back and found Kepha standing outside the door. Therefore, Yowchanan spoke to the gate warden and introduced Kepha and the gate warden allowed Kepha to enter into the open courtyard. Yowchanan rushed inside where Yahusha was taken while Kepha stayed in the open courtyard.

Kaiaphas and the invited members of the Sanhedrin sought untrue testimony against Yahusha so that they could kill Him. However, no evidence could be found against Him yet many bearers of untrue testimony as illegitimate witnesses were approaching. Eventually, two came near saying, "This one said I am able to demolish the Temple of Yahuah and after three days construct it!" Kaiaphas stood up and addressed Yahusha, "Do You respond nothing of what these testify against You?" But Yahusha remained hushed and refused to speak. Then one of the *Parash* (Pharasee's) exclaimed, "I exact an oath to You by the living Yahuah that You speak words to us, if You are *HaMachiach ben Yahuah* (the Anointed Messiah, son of Yahuah)." Yahusha looked up and replied, "I talked publicly with frankness to the world. I at all times taught in the synagogue of the assemblage of persons and in the temple at which spot the *Yhuwdiy* (Hebrew's) at all times convened together and I talked about nothing concealed to privacy. Why do you inquire of Me? Ask those having heard what words I uttered to them! Without question, these know what I said." Immediately, one of the temple guards holding Yahusha captive, slapped Yahusha with a stinging blow across His mouth saying, "In this way, you respond to the *Gadowl Kohen* (High Priest)?" Yahusha responded to the guard, "If I talked in a bad way, be a witness and testify with respect to the evil. But if I spoke well, why do you thrash Me?" The agitated and embarrassed High Priest then screamed, "Speak plainly! Are You *HaMachiach ben Yahuah* (the Anointed Messiah, son of Yahuah)?" Yahusha looked straight into the eyes of Kaiaphas and said, "You spoke it. Yet, I relate to you in words, from now on you will see the Son of Man sitting off to the right of miraculous power and coming on the clouds of heaven, the eternal abode of Yahuah."

At that instant in time, the chief priest tore asunder his outer dress laying forth words, "He spoke impiously against Yahuah! Why do we still need to require continuation of witnesses? Lo, now you heard the vilification against Yahuah! What do you think?" Some of the members of the Sanhedrin began to scream, "Mavet! Mavet! (Death! Death!)" Then the temple guards grabbed the hair on the back of the head of Yahusha to hold His face upright as members of the Sanhedrin walked by and spit in His face. As the thick mucus of the Parash (Pharisees) drooled down His beard and face, the Messiah did not flinch or protest. When the Pharisees were through with their disgraceful actions then the temple guards holding him began to beat Him violently with their fists. The blows stung His already beaten body adding stinging pain to His bruised ribs and swollen and black and blue face. Then they blindfolded His eyes and slapped Him sending a lasting stinging sensation into the depths of His swollen cheeks and lips. They taunted Him saying, "Speak under inspiration to us, Anointed Messiah! Who is that hitting You violently like the sting of a scorpion?"

In the meantime, outside in the open courtyard of the mansion belonging to *HaGadowl Kohen* (the High Priest), as the trial was taking place inside, *Kepha* (Peter) had sat down to warm himself from the night's chilly air with the yellow-glowing fire from the bed of red-hot burning coals, which had been lit in the middle of the yard open to the wind. Then a servant girl of Kaiaphas approached and came near to him. She sat down near the light of the fire and gazed intently at him and said, "You were with Yahusha the *Galiylah'iy* (Galilean)!" But he rejected and disavowed the claim in front of all blasting, "Woman, I do not know what you are relating in words!" Then he hastily issued out into the gateway of the building which was an alley way vestibule of the forecourt and a cock emitted a crowing sound. While in this place, a different servant girl who was a relative of *Melek* (Malchus) the one whom Kepha had amputated his ear in the Garden saw him and exclaimed, "This one was with Yahusha the *Nazoraios* (Nazarene) in the Garden!" Once again Kepha rejected and disavowed the claim except this time with a sacred oath growling, "I do not know that human being!"

After an hour had intervened, Yahusha was being led outside to be taken to the jail of the mansion of the High Priest. Then some of those standing near to Kepha began to look at him through the light of the fire. They approached and came near to Kepha as they pointed in the direction of the Messiah said to him, "Truly, you also are one of them, even because of the accent of your talking makes you clear." Then he began to call down a curse and to declare another sacred oath under penalty of being consumed by the evilness of Satan screaming, "I said that I do not know that retched human being! I would not be caught dead with that man! Now leave me alone!" At that instant Yahusha twisted around and stared into the eyes of Kepha. That very instant in time, for a second time, a cock emitted the sound of crowing. Kepha then bore in mind and recollected the utterance on the matter of Yahusha, Who had said, *"Prior to a cock emitting the sound of crowing twice, you will deny utterly and disown Me three times!"* So, Kepha now distraught sent himself away outside the complex walls and he sobbed and wailed out loud bitterly with violence. As he reflected on what had just taken place, thoughts raced bitterly through his mind. How could he deny "The Master"? How could he steep so low to disavow and curse *haben Yahuah* (the Son of Yahuah)?" How could he betray the unwavering love of Yahusha for him?"

As the dawn of Wednesday morning came into being, the *gadowl kohen's* (high priests) all took advisement in a deliberative body along with the senior members of the Sanhedrin of the people against Yahusha, so as to kill Him. After the decision on what to do, they bound Him once again, removed Him from the jail of the mansion and they took Him off and surrendered Him to *Pontios Pilatos* (Pontius Pilate) the governor and chief of the province of Yhuwdah (Judea). When Yhuwdah Shim'own Iysh'Qriyowth (Judas Simon Iscariot), the one that yielded up the Messiah, saw Him bound and being led to Pilate because Yahusha had been sentenced and judged against, Yhuwdah (Judas) cared afterwards and regretted what he had done.

So, he took the thirty pieces of silver cash being drachma's by weight of the shekel (12 ounces of silver valued at $4.90) back to the high priests and the senior members of the Sanhedrin before they left the Temple. He said to them, "I missed the mark and sinned by yielding up blood that was not guilty!" One of the high priests replied, "What is that to us? You gaze upon what you did with open eyes!" Then Yhuwdah (Judas) spit on the brown skin bag containing the thirty pieces of silver as a sign of contempt and he flung them at the high priests with a quick toss and the pieces of silver began falling to the Temple floor jingling as they fell from the air onto the marble floor. He quickly ran out of the Temple and he began to see demonic faces tormenting and laughing at him. He ran through the Lower City of Yruwshalaim (Jerusalem), and exited the city walls through the southeast gate *Sha'ar HaAshpot* known as the Dung Gate. He traveled a short distance to Potter's Field where the pottery makers would dig clay to make their pottery and strangled himself to death by hanging from a tree.

Later on the *gadowl kohen's* (high priests) learned of the news of what Yhuwdah Shim'own Iysh'Qriyowth (Judas Simon Iscariot) had done to himself so they took the silver cash and said, "It is not right being out in public to place these pieces of silver back into the offering of the Temple fund since it is the money paid for blood." After taking advisement from a deliberative body, they purchased the Field of the Potter to be used for the burial of foreign guests. Thus that field in the country was called *Haeldama* (The Field of Blood) even until this day. At that time, what was poured forth through the inspired prophet, Zkaryah (Zechariah) chapter eleven verses twelve and thirteen relating in words, "***I took the thirty silver pieces of cash, the money paid for the One Whom the valuation was fixed upon, Whom they fixed the valuation upon from the sons of Yishra'Yah and gave them for the field in the country of the potter as Yahuah had directed me.***"

The large wooden double-gate of the Praetorian Palace opened as a dozen praetorian guards stood watch overhead on the walkway above the gates. The four guards who had opened the gates stood at the end of each gate two on each side, dressed in full battle armor with their red plumage on their helmets glistening in the early morning dawn light. The large wooden double gates opened to a huge open courtyard which terminated at the dozens of steps leading up to the platform and judgment throne of Pilot. Half a dozen praetorian guards stood at the base of the steps with two more guards standing on each side of the throne. The *gadowl kohen's* (high priests) entered first into the large open courtyard under the very watchful eyes of the praetorian guards. Following the *gadowl kohen's* (high priests) were the Temple guards escorting the bound Yahusha. Last to enter the large open courtyard of the Praetorian Palace was an enormous crowd that had gathered which filled the courtyard to overflowing capacity spilling out of the large wooden double gates into the street. The Hebrews gathered in the outer courtyard instead of the great judgment hall of the governor's courtroom so that they not be contaminated, keeping themselves clean in order that they could eat the *Pecach* (Passover). After the enormous crowd packed themselves into the open courtyard like sardines, *Pontios Pilatos* (Governor Pontius Pilate) appeared on the praetorian platform and the crowd began to murmur their dislike for the Roman Governor.

Pilate raised his arms and silenced the crowd. He then directed his conversation directly towards Kaiaphas (Caiaphas) the chief high priest by questioning, "Kaiaphas why do you trouble me at this hour of the early morning? Do you not have a festival to prepare for today?" Kaiaphas responded, "*S'likha Moshel* (Excuse me Governor) we bring a pressing and serious matter before you today! We bring to you a prisoner that has broken our Torah" At that moment the

Temple guards shoved Yahusha in front of the pious high priests so Pilate could see Him. Pilate was taken aback and remarked, "Why have you brought Him to me? It looks as if you have already punished Him. Do you treat all your prisoners suspected of wrong-doing this way before being sentenced to guilt?" Then the huge overflowing crowd broke out in spontaneous laughter. This angered Kaiaphas so he spun on his heels and faced the crowd with raised arms shouting, "*Sheket! Sheket!* (Quiet! Quiet!)"

When the overflowing crowd became somewhat silent once again, Kaiaphas turned back around and addressed Pilate saying, "*S'likha. S'likha bevakasha Moshel!* (Excuse me. Excuse me please, Governor!" Pilate replied, "*Quid Vis!* (What do you want?) What complaint of a criminal charge do you bring against this Man?" Kaiaphas responded and said to him, "Unless this One was not a criminal then we would not have yielded Him up to you." Then Pilate said to him, "You take Him and judicially condemn and punish Him according to your Mosaic Law." Then one of the high priest yelled, "It is not right being out in public for us to put anyone to death!" Kaiaphas explained and began to charge Him with some offences, saying, "We found this one distorting and corrupting our nation and preventing to give to Kaiser (Caesar) toll taxes and expressing Himself that He Exists as the Messiah, a Sovereign! Governor we ask that you question the prisoner and you will also find Him to be a criminal."

Then *Pontios Pilatos* (Governor Pontius Pilate) motioned for a couple of the praetorian guards to bring Yahusha up the steps to him. Pilate removed himself inside the portico a little way to question Yahusha in private as Yahusha was being brought up the steps to him. When Yahusha arrived Pilate offered Him a cup of water but Yahusha refused the cooling drink.

2

As Yahusha stood in front of Pilate, the chief of the province, Pilate inquired and questioned Him laying forth words, "Are You the Sovereign of the Yhudiy (Jews)?" Yahusha said, "You related it in words." However, as for the charges of the offence of Him by the high priests and the senior members of the Sanhedrin, He did not respond. At that time *Pontios Pilatos* (Pontius Pilate) related in words to Him, "Do you not hear what they testify against You?" But He did not respond to even one utterance in order that the chief of the province was greatly filled with admiration.

Pontios Pilatos (Pontius Pilate) pondered the situation for a long moment because of personal past conflicts with the high priests he knew their evil hearts so he returned to the platform and said to the *gadowl kohen's* (high priests) and the throng of rabble, "I do not find a crime in this Man!" But they insisted more fiercely, laying forth words, "He excites the people, teaching all Yhuwdah, commencing in *Galiylah* (Galilee) then from *Galiylah* (Galilee) to here in this spot!" When *Pilatos* heard *Galiylah*, he inquired privately of Yahusha if He was a *Galiylah'iy* (Galilean). Having recognized that He was from the jurisdiction of *Herodes Antipater* (Herod Antipas), he sent Him up to Herod, he also being in Yruwshalaim (Jerusalem) during those days of the festival.

Herodes Antipater (Herod Antipas) was in his throne chamber when Yahusha was brought before him by the praetorian guards followed closely by the *gadowl kohen's* (high priests). Herod saw Yahusha and be became cheerful and happy and ordered his servant to bring him another cup of wine. For this reason, he was wishing for a long time to see Him, because of hearing many things about Him. Herod was expecting some supernatural indication to see come into being by Him. He inquired of Him with many words but Yahusha did not respond to him. Therefore, the high priests and scribes stood and fiercely charged Him with some offences. Having despised Him, they made Him out to be utterly nothing. Then Herod also with his body of troops jeered at and derided Him. Finally, Herod at the dismay of the high priests, placed on Yahusha radiant and magnificent clothing fit for a ruler and sent Him back to *Pilatos*. Both Pilate and Herod became friends on that same day with one another. For this reason, they existed previously in hostility between themselves because of political ruling envy but now were united standing against the cause of the high priests.

The praetorian guards escorted Yahusha back to *Pontios Pilatos* (Pontius Pilate) and he convoked together the high priests and the first in rank of the Hebrews and said to them, "You brought to me this Man as turning away the people and lo, I have interrogated, investigated and scrutinized Him in front of you and in private and found nothing to be a reason for a crime in this Man of which you charge against Him with offenses. Neither did Herodes who sent this document back stating, "For this reason, I send Him back to you and lo, nothing deserving of death has been done by Him." The high priests stirred the overflowing crowd to begin to grumble and become restless. In order that what Yahusha had said about Himself being the Messiah could verify the prediction which He said indicating what sort of death He was about to die. Therefore, Pilate directed the praetorian guards to put up a line of defense with battle gear drawn in front of the crowd. Pilate entered into the Praetorian the great judgment hall of the governor's court room once more and called for Yahusha to be brought to him.

Pilate looked sternly at Yahusha and asked, "I ask you once again, are you the Sovereign of the Yhuwdiy (Jews)?" Yahusha responded, "Do you express this from yourself or did different ones speak this to you with respect to Me?" *Pilatos* defended his question and said, "I am not a Yhuwd (Jew)! Your own nation and the high priests yielded You up to me! What did You do?" Yahusha who had until this point kept His head bowed and looked at the floor, raised his chin up and looked towards the heavens and answered, "My royalty, realm and rule is not of this world. My assistants would have struggled and fought My enemies in order that I would not be yielded up to the Yhuwdiy (Jews) leaders. But now My royalty, realm and rule is not from here." Accordingly, Pilatos said to Him, "Are You not really a Sovereign?" Yahusha replied, "You express that I EXIST as a Sovereign. I have been born for this thing and for this thing I have come into the world in order that I could be a witness and testify to the truth. Everyone who is of the truth hears My voice." Piilatos expressed to Him, "What is truth?" After hearing this he issued out once more to the Yhuwdiy leaders and crowd and pronounced to them, "I found not even one crime in Him! There is a mutual habituation to you that I should free fully to you at the Pecach (Passover). Certainly, you will who I should free fully to you. Do you choose the Sovereign of the Yhuwdiy?"

You see at the festival of Pecach (Passover) it was the habit of the chief of the province to free fully and dismiss one bound captive to the throng of rabble whoever they chose. At that time, they had a remarkable bound captive named Yahusha Bar-abba (Yahusha the son of Abba). He had been found with the insurgents, who during the public uprising committed murder. Since the crowd was already convened together, Pilatos said to them, "Whom do you wish that I should free fully and dismiss for you, Yahusha Bar-abba or Yahusha called Anointed Messiah?" For this reason Pilate knew that because of ill will and the jealousy of spite the Yhuwdiy (Jewish) leaders had surrendered Him up. Then Pilatos sat down on the rostrum for a tribunal. Just as he sat down a servant boy brought a little scroll and gave it to Pilate. His wife had sent a message to him concerning Yahusha, laying forth words, "You do nothing to that One innocent in character and holy in actions! For this reason, I experienced a painful sensation today by a dream because of Him!"

However, the *gadowl kohen's* (High Priests) and the senior members of the Sanhedrin convinced the throng of rabble that they should ask for Bar-abba and to destroy fully Yahusha. The chief of the province, Pilate, said to the overflowing crowd, "Which do you choose from the two that I should free fully to you?" The crowd yelled, "Bar-abba!" Pilatos laid forth words to them, "What then should I do to Yahusha called Anointed Messiah?" The overflowing crowd cheered on by the high priests began to scream, "*Mut! Mut! Mut!* (Death! Death! Death!) Then Pilatos quieted the crowd as tension grew between the praetorian guards and the restless crowd. Pilate asked once again, "For what reason, what worthless and depraved injury has He done? I will punish Him and release Him." But the crowd became unruly and croaked like a screaming ravens shrieking more loudly, laying froth bitter words, "*Mavet mishpat* (Death sentence))! Let Him be impaled on a cross!"

Because of the rowdy crowd, Pilate sentenced Yahusha to be scourged. To be scourged was to be whipped with an instrument called the "cat-o'-nine-tails." This special whip had nine strands of long leather braided with metal balls and containing embedded pieces of razor-sharp metal between each metal ball. The metal balls were the size of large marbles and would cause deep contusions (bruises) which would break open after repeated blows upon the naked skin. The purpose of the razor sharp pieces of metal was to filet the flesh causing deep cuts. The back of the victim would be so shredded that part of the spine would sometimes be exposed due to the deep cuts in the flesh.

In addition the Roman beatings by scourging caused lacerations (cutting of the flesh) that would tear into the underlying skeletal muscles and produce quivering ribbons of bleeding flesh. Even the victim's veins were open to exposure. This type of whipping caused the victim's body to go into hypovolemic shock. Thus the heart would race to pump blood that wasn't there, the blood pressure would drop and result in fainting. Then the kidney's would stop producing urine in order to maintain what volume was left in the body causing the person to experience extreme thirst as the body craved fluids to replace the lost blood volume. The beatings went all the way from the shoulders to the back, down the buttocks and the back of the legs. The Romans reserved this cruel and usually deadly punishment for murderers and traitors.

Yahusha was stripped naked of all His clothes and His bare feet were shackled to the bottom of a hitching post. Then His hands were put in iron cuffs which were chained to a pulley above and His naked body was stretched until the bare skin on His body was tight so that the barbs of the cat-o'-nine-tails could cut deeply when the blows were inflicted. Two strong muscular soldiers were assigned to administer the whipping, one on each side of Yahusha. This was so that each blow could be given with maximum force without the soldier becoming completely exhausted.

Both soldiers watched intently for the Roman commander to drop his hand as a signal to begin the scourging. A crowd of curious onlookers, cheap thrill-seekers and members of the Parash gathered to watch the public infliction of punishment upon the Messiah. A Roman soldier acting as a messenger unrolled a sealed scroll in front of the face of the Roman commander. After the commander had read the scroll he yelled in a loud voice, "*Triginta nuvem* (Thirty-nine)!" Meaning the Messiah was to receive thirty-nine lashes. The air grew thick with tension as everyone was waiting with baited breath for the commander to drop his hand.

What the onlookers could not see was the amassing of hideous black bat-like creatures with beady glowing red eyes and long sharp vampire teeth drooling with acidic saliva. The dark lord Satan had assigned them to feast upon the flesh of the Messiah like a flock of starving vultures. The large black wings of the Vulture of Death extended over the city of Yruwshalaim (Jerusalem) as its sharp talons clung to the pinnacle of the Great Temple of Yahuah as it remembered the first Pecach (Passover) of death of the first-born in the country of Mitsrayim (Egypt) many years ago that led to the freedom of the Hebrew nation from the slavery of Pharaoh. Now the greatest Passover Lamb was about to be sacrificed and they were ready for a banquet of vengeance.

The hand of the Roman commander began to unexpectedly quiver and the Vulture of Death let out a blood-curdling screech that even shook the black boiling cauldron of Satan in the demonic world of Hades. At that moment in time the Roman commander dropped his hand and nodded his head as the first executioner drew the whip back over his shoulder and with a fully extended arm threw all his weight and strength into the whip across the bare shoulder of Yahusha. The smack of the leather whip could be heard throughout the courtyard as the metal barbs pierced the bare flesh of the Messiah. When the executioner jerked back the imbedded whip blood began to ooze out of the pierced flesh of the Messiah's shoulder. The Roman military recording secretary yelled, "*Unus* (One)"and the evil bat-like spirit demons flocked to the body of Yahusha. They hovered over His bound body impatiently waiting for raw flesh to appear. The Roman secretary yelled, "*duo* (two)" and the second executioner drew his whip over his shoulder and with full force came down upon the bare flesh of the Messiah. Once again the dull thud of the leather smacked against the naked body of Yahusha and the sharp barbs dug into his flesh causing small lacerations where the barbs had embedded themselves into His flesh.

This scene repeated itself over and over and over again. The secretary yelled, "*tres…quattuor…quinque… sex….septem…octo…novem…decem…* (three, four, five, six, seven, eight, nine, ten)." Now the upper shoulders and back of the Messiah began to look like raw ground hamburger. The bat-like demons attacked the raw bleeding flesh of the Messiah sinking their vampire teeth into His blood. As soon as their long sharp teeth touched His blood, it became rays of burning light and the bat-like minions of Satan whimpered and shrieked out in severe tormenting pain. After a few attempts of attacking the Messiah's bleeding raw body they abandoned their futile mission and as they tried to retreat in failure back to Hades in defeat the huge Vulture of Death picked them out of the air one by one and consumed them using the strength of their spirits to become stronger itself.

Once again the non-stop counting continued to be heard in the courtyard, "*undecim…duodecim…tredecim….quattuordecim…quindecim…..sedecim….septendecim….duodeviginti…undeviginti…..viginti…* (eleven, twelve, thirteen, fourteen, fifteen, sixteen, seventeen, eighteen, nineteen, twenty). The shoulders, entire back, buttocks, and upper legs of the Messiah were a bloody raw unrecognizable flesh. Even though the executioners were beginning to tire somewhat His flesh was so raw that now they were yanking off chunks of bleeding quivering ribbons of raw flesh from His body. Below His body was nothing but a pond of crimson red blood. The Messiah's body now hung limp exhausted from the severe trauma inflicted upon His naked body. Yahusha focused not on the intense pain throbbing throughout His body but instead upon doing Yahuah's will. Therefore, He knew that He was fulfilling prophecy by the ancient prophet *Ysha'Yah* (Isaiah) chapter fifty-three verses three through five.

53:3-5, *"Disesteemed, destitute and rejected by men, a son of anguish from affliction and known of malady and anxiety. Also as keeping secret of faces from Him. Being disesteemed and we did not value or regard Him. Surely our maladies, anxieties and calamities He has born and our anguish from affliction He carried them. But we did not regard or value Him, violently struck and punished being stricken severely by Yahuah and afflicted. But He was wounded by boring through Him for our religious and moral revolt, cracked to pieces for our perverse evil. The chastisement as a warning and instruction of our peace was on Him. With His stripes and welts and black and blue marks we ourselves are mended and cured."*

At this moment in time, many of the curious spectators had left because they could not bear to see the brutality and inhumane scourging inflicted upon the bound and captive Messiah. Even the spiteful and jealous high priests could not bear to witness any more of this brutal activity. The worst of animals had never received such horrific treatment. As the counting continued more and more spectators would leave back to the streets shaking their heads in disbelief. Those Roman soldiers in attendance began to shout encouragement to the two executioners as the counting continued, "*viginti unus...viginti duo...viginti tres...viginti quattuor...viginti quinque... viginti ses...viginti septem...viginti octo...viginti novem...triginta...*(twenty-one, twenty-two, twenty-three, twenty-four, twenty-five, twenty-six, twenty-seven, twenty-eight, twenty-nine, thirty).

Now the executioners were breathing very hard with their chests heaving up and down and trying to rest between each alternating blow by putting their hands on their hips. Their military uniformed bodies were covered with spattered blood and raw flesh. Their faces were blushed with exhaustion and smeared with the blood of the Messiah. No matter how exhausted they were, the counting did not stop and the fierceness of their effort to fillet the flesh from the Messiah's naked body did not wane. The Roman secretary yelled, "*Triginta unus* (thirty-one)" and the executioner obliged and swung the devastating instrument of punishment upon the body wrapping the barbs clear around the side upon the chest of the Messiah.

Again, "*Triginta duo* (thirty-two)" yelled the counting secretary as the second executioner swung his whip and ripped another chunk of raw flesh off the naked body of Yahshua. "*Triginta tres* (thirty-three)... *Triginta quattuor* (thirty-four)...*Triginta quinque* (thirty-five)...*Triginta sex* (thirty-six)...*Triginta septem* (thirty-seven)...*Triginta octo* (thirty-eight)...*Triginta novem* (thirty-nine)." The Roman commander then gave the cease signal and the executioners dropped their whips of cat-o'-nine-tails and put their hands on their knees heaving up and down trying to get oxygen in their exhausted bodies.

While the two exhausted executioners were trying to catch their breath, two fresh Roman soldiers walked over to the taunt pulley and released the pressure allowing the Messiah to crash to the cobblestone pavement in a crumpled heap of raw bleeding flesh splashing in the pool of His own blood that had accumulated under His battered body during the brutal infliction of pain and suffering. Then the two fresh soldiers unlocked the cold steel shackles bound to the black and blue bruised ankles of Yahusha. The Roman Commander gave a brushing off move with his hand in the direction of the two fresh Roman soldiers. Each soldier grabbed a bloody wrist of the Messiah and began to drag Him with His raw and bleeding back scraping across the rough cobblestone pavement towards the brigade of the Praetorian.

At that time, the warriors of the chief of the province, having received near Yahusha in the brigade of the Praetorian and collected against Him all the mass of the Roman military men. They propped Him up against a wall of the brigade and placed around His naked body a crimson colored military cloak. One of the Roman soldiers taunted, "What do we have here, a sovereign without a crown?" This brought laughter and additional deriding comments from the other soldiers present. Then the Roman soldier stepped back outside the brigade for a while and then came back inside having braided a crown of three-inch thorns holding them very carefully with the end of his military cloak. Next he placed it with hostility upon the head of Yahusha pushing it with a reed until it pricked the scalp and forehead of the Messiah causing slow trickles of blood to flow down His face and also in His hair. Then the soldier took the reed that was used to push on the crown of thorns and put it upon His right hand. The soldiers continued to ridicule the Messiah with hostility as they fell on the knee in front of Him and they jeered at and derided Him laying forth words, "Be well, sovereign of the Yhudiy!" They also spit on Him and took the reed and thumped with repeated blows the crown of thorns on His head. One of the on looking Roman soldiers grabbed his own head and began crying out, "*Heu vae! Heu vae! Heu vae!* (Woe is me! Woe is me! Woe is me!) This disgusting mockery produced additional laughter from the Roman soldiers watching the suffering Messiah being used as a form of entertainment. Then the Chief Roman Commander of the Praetorian Guard appeared and halted the despicable circus and ordered that Yahusha be taken immediately back to Pilate.

Pilate once again issued outdoors and appeared on the rostrum and quieted the overflowing crowd and said to them, "Behold, I am bringing Him outdoors to you that you may know that I find not even one crime alleged or proven in Him." Two Roman soldiers assisted Yahusha outdoors to the rostrum wearing the burden of the thorny wreath and the scarlet military cloak. His appearance was unrecognizable with His hair matted with dried blood, His face disfigured and His body covered with deep open lacerations. When the crowd saw Him there was a collective gasp and His women followers began to weep. Pilate yelled, "Behold the Man!" When the *gadowl kohens* (chief priests) and the officers of the Sanhedrin saw that the Messiah had gained the sympathy of the crowd they immediately clamored and cried out, "*Mavet! Mavet!* (Death! Death!)" Pilate now being agitated yelled back at the *Yhudiy* (Jewish) leaders, "Take Him yourselves and impale Him on the cross. For this reason I did not find a crime in Him."

One of the legal scribes responded to Pilate, "We possess a law and according to the *Torah* (Mosaic Law), He is under obligation to die because He has made Himself to be *HaBen Yahuah* (The Son of Yahuah)!" Certainly, when Pilatos heard what was just said, he was frightened and entered into the Praetorian, the great judgment hall of the governor's courtroom and ordered the Roman soldiers to escort Yahusha in to him. Pilatos once more expressed to Yahusha, "Where are You from?" But Yahusha did not give him a response. Accordingly, Pilatos questioned Him, "You do not talk to me? Do you not know that I possess the freedom of delegated influence to

23

release you?" Yahusha looked up with blood stained and swollen eyelids and mustered all the strength to speak which was a broken loud whisper, "You would not possess the freedom of delegated influence, not even one thing against Me if it was not given to you from above. Therefore, the one that yielded Me up to you possesses a greater sin."

From out of this Pilatos returned once again outdoors in front of the overflowing crowd and sought to pardon and release Him but the Yhuwdi (Jews) shrieked and screamed like croaking ravens laying forth words, "If you release, this One you are not a friend of *Kaisar* (Caesar). Anyone making Himself a sovereign disputes *Kaisar* (Caesar)!" Accordingly, Pilatos heard what was said and brought Yahusha back outdoors in front of His people, the overflowing crowd. Pilatos then sat down on the tribunal judgment seat on the rostrum at a location called The Pavement, meaning "Stone-strewed" being inlaid with multicolored stones in geometrical figures on which the Roman tribunal was placed but in Hebrew it was called *Gabbuwth* meaning "lofty pride".

It was Wednesday the Day of readiness of the *Pecach* (Passover) the fourteenth day of *Nissan* (March-April) and the third hour (nine o'clock a.m.) would soon be approaching so Pilatos tried once again and pleaded with the crowd, "Lo, your Sovereign." This stirred up the crowd and Yhuwdiy (Jewish) leaders to a high pitch almost being riotous and they clamored, "Take Him away, take Him away, impale Him on the cross!" Pilatos asked, "Should I impale on the cross your Sovereign?" The *gadowl kohens* (High Priests) screamed like croaking ravens, "We do not have a Sovereign except *Kaisar* (Caesar)!" At this point the crowd led by the high priests began to push against the Roman guards forming a line of protection at the bottom of the steps leading up to the rostrum. At once, the Head of the Praetorian Guard called in reinforcements tripling the military presence at the bottom of the steps in addition to having archers poised with drawn bows in the towers and the catwalks. A look of anxiety blanked the Captain's face as he looked back at Pilatos for additional orders for action.

Pilate saw that nothing was being useful or benefitting but rather a disturbance was coming into being. So, he took water and he washed off his own hands in front of the throng of rabble, relating in words as a set discourse, "I am not guilty of the blood of this One innocent in character and holy in actions. You will gaze with wide-open eyes at something remarkable." All the people responded saying, "His blood is on us and our children!" Therefore at that time, Pilate freed fully and dismissed to them Yahusha Bar-abba and Yahusha *HaMachiach* (the Anointed) was led away to the brigade to be transmitted in order that He could be impaled on the cross to extinguish the passion of the crowd.

The overflowing crowd began to make their way from the large outdoor courtyard through the large wooden double gates as the Messiah was led by the Roman soldiers back to the brigade. There to greet Yahusha was a cohort (numbering around three hundred) of soldiers who promptly began deriding and jeering at Him. After a few moments of verbal abuse, when they had finished jeering at and deriding Him, they stripped off the military cloak from Him and put on Him His own clothing, the one-piece tunic shirt and His outside cloak. The Captain of the Guard entered the brigade and yelled, "*Contendunt sursum!* (Hurry up!) This is to be completed before *plein midi* (high noon). Get the other two prisoners in here now!" At that moment, the blood-stained and severely wounded legs of the Messiah still being weak from the brutal and barbaric whipping He endured, gave way and He crumpled to the floor. This prompted the two soldiers guarding Him to begin to give Him some swift kicks yelling,

"*Erigo! Exurgo!* (Get up! Stand up!)" The Roman Captain pointed his finger at the two soldiers and commanded in a harsh tone, "*Sistite! Sistite!* (Stop! Stop!)"

A few moments later, eight armed Roman soldiers appeared from the belly of the Praetorian Palace, the dungeon where the criminals were kept, with the other two prisoners who were also to be crucified with the Messiah. The first one was middle-aged with a filthy straggly beard and a very foul mouth as he continually barraged and harangued the Roman soldiers with foul cursing. The second was in his early twenties and more reserved. As soon as he saw Yahusha, he spit at one of the Roman soldiers and screamed, "*Barbariy khayaim!* (Barbaric animals!)" This prompted him to receive a quick punch with the wooden handle of the soldier's spear to the back of his head which knocked him down to the floor. In turn while he was on the floor the soldier also kicked him in the ribs and yelled, "*Exurgo!* (Stand up!)" His eyes met the eyes of the Messiah and as he stood up. Then the Messiah also struggled up to stand upright on His feet.

The other two prisoners had their hands untied briefly while a *patibulum* (crossbar) was tied to each of their arms as it was laid across the back of their shoulders. Once the two prisoners were secured, three soldiers placed the *patibulum* (crossbar) across the bloodied and raw shoulders of Yahusha. They started to secure His arms to the ruff wooden crossbar with rough burlap ropes but the Roman Captain ordered, "*Minime!* (No!)". Then the Captain ordered for his horse to be brought to him. He put his leg in the stirrup and settled in the leather saddle. At the nod of his shiny brass helmet decorated with a red brush-like crest on its top running down the center of the helmet, the door to the street was opened up and the two-thousand foot journey from the Antonia Fortress to Calvary began on the street called *Dolorosa* meaning "suffering".

3

So the death march began on the cobblestone pavement which would lead past the Antonia Fortress towards the northwest gate known as the Damascus Gate or in Hebrew *Sha'ar Sh'khem* (Gate of Shechem). The Damascus Gate was comprised of two large fortified wooden gates and was a very busy entrance into the fortified city of Yruwshalaim (Jerusalem). Entering this gate from the outside lead straight to the Sheep Gate of the Temple about fifteen hundred feet due south where the one year old lambs were taken for sacrifice. Exiting from the inside of the Damascus Gate led to a hill known as *Gulgoleth* (Golgotha) in the Hebrew language meaning "Place of the Skull". This hill along the main road from the north was where the Romans preferred to hold their crucifixions to serve as a warning to all those who passed by entering and exiting the city.

Not too far up the dusty road from the Damascus Gate traveling to the Great City of Yruwshalaim (Jerusalem) was *Shim'own* (Simon) from a field of a country farm located near the city known in the Greek language as *Kuren* (Cyrene) the capital city of Cyrenaica (Libya, North Africa). He along with his two very young sons, *Alexandros* (Alexander) age eight and curly red-haired *Rhouphos* (Rufus) age six, were headed to the great city to participate in the *Pecach* (Passover). As they walked on the road towards the Damascus Gate of the city of Yruwshalaim (Jerusalem) the two small sons walked beside him as they led a one year old lamb. The main reason *Shim'own* (Simon) brought his two young sons so far from home was to watch the lamb.

As they neared the great wooden gates of the Damascus Gate, the curly black haired talkative *Alexandros* (Alexander) asked, "*Ab, Ab* (Father, father) what is the great city like? There's so much that we don't know." So *Shim'own* (Simon) quickly told them about *Mosheh* (Moses) and the patriarchs and then he said, "Boys above all you must watch the lamb. The crowds will be so big in *Yruwshalaim* (Jerusalem) that you must be sure the lamb doesn't get loose and run away."

Shim'own (Simon) and his two young boys tugging on the rope leading the lamb entered the wooden gates of the Damascus Gate and when they had traveled half the distance to the Sheep Gate belonging to the Temple, *Shim'own* (Simon) knew something was wrong. He could not hear any joyful worshippers or no joyful worship songs in the streets. So he stood there with his small boys among angry men. At a far distance they heard the angry mob cry "Crucify Him." He grabbed his young sons by the shoulders and tried to go against the crowd but they could not escape. They were forced to participate in this drama against their will. The terrified little boys clung tightly to their father whose thoughts were racing in his mind, "Why this very day were men condemned to die? Why are we forced to be here near where the condemned would pass by soon?"

As the captain on the horse led the prisoners though the street of *Dolorosa* the armed Roman soldiers tried to keep the pushing crowd back at bay so that there would be a clear path. They also would whip the backs of the prisoners including Yahusha the Messiah or jab them with the blunt end of their spear handle if they began to walk too slow and not keep up the pace with the captain on the horse. Along the way the crowd spat on the prisoners and threw rotten fruit and vegetables as they hurled abusive curse words towards the ears of the maligned and condemned prisoners.

Shim'own (Simon) looked over the heads of the rowdy and angry crowd and could see them coming very near. The first prisoner begged for mercy but the second one was violent, arrogant and loud. *Shim'own* (Simon) and his little boys could hear his angry voice screaming obscenities at the crowd. Then someone near *Shim'one* (Simon) said, "Here comes Yahusha!" *Shim'own* (Simon) could hardly believe what he saw. In front of him was a man so badly beaten that He appeared almost dead. Blood oozed from his entire body and from the thorns on His head. The blood ran off the patibulum for the cross to the ground. He watched Him as He struggled to walk and carry the heavy wooden beam. Then he watched Him as He fell and the heavy beam came down upon His brutalized back. The soldiers began to whip Yahusha and kick Him in the sides. In that moment *Shim'own* (Simon) could hear his sobbing little boys and felt great emotional pain as the hateful crowd continued to yell. He and his sons were trapped and he felt hopeless.

Then a Roman soldier grabbed his arm and screamed, "Hey you! Carry His cross!" With his young sons crying hysterically and clinging tightly to his garment at first he tried to resist the solder but the soldier reached for his long silver sword. Those nearby in the crowd pried the two frightened boys away from *Shim'own* (Simon), he looked back but could not see his sons who were now lost in the mob-like crowd. Therefore, he knelt down and took the heavy wooden beam from the Messiah and placed it upon his own shoulders and started down the street. The blood that Yahusha had been shedding began to run down his own cheek.

The large throng of people continued to follow behind the death march and the women along the sides of the procession were beating their breasts in grief and bewailing the Messiah. Yahusha twisted His head around and said, "Daughters of Yruwshalaim (Jerusalem) do not sob and wail loudly over Me but sob out loud for yourselves and for your children. Lo, because days will come in which they will say supremely blest are the sterile and the matrix cavities which did not give birth and the breasts that did not suckle the nipple. Then they will lay forth words to the mountains, 'Fall on us!' and to the hillocks 'Cover us up!' Because if they do these things when a tree is wet with fresh sap, what may come into being in the scorching and arid earth without water?" What seemed like an eternity they soon were outside the Damascus Gate and trudged up the hill where the poles of capital punishment were awaiting their victims.

When they had reached the top of the hill of *Gulgoleth* (Golgotha) the captain on the prancing horse halted the procession and the soldiers pushed the prisoners down to the ground. *Shim'own* (Simon) was huffing and puffing and dropped the patibulum off his shoulders and it made a dull thud as it hit the ground raising a small cloud of dust. Then a soldier pushed him backwards away from Yahusha towards the crowd and he lost his balance not expecting the shove and he landed on his back with the back of his head crashing hard onto the rocky hill. A couple of onlookers in the crowd that had followed the procession helped him up with his blood stained cloak and face. Each of the prisoners were stripped completely naked and were given gall with its greenish hue being poison of wormwood. However, having tasted it, Yahusha refused to drink the pain killer. This was predicted in the Scriptures of the Holy Writ in the book of *Thillahyim* (Psalms) chapter sixty-nine verses twenty through twenty-two, **"You know My disgrace of having My sexual organs exposed and My shame and My disgrace. Before you are all My adversaries. This disgrace of having My sexual organs exposed has burst to pieces My heart and I am sick. I looked for consolation but received none and for**

My consolers and I found none. They gave Me in my food the poison poppy plant of gall and in My thirst they gave Me to drink vinegar."

Then two soldiers tied ruff burlap ropes around each forearm of the Messiah and as they stretched out His arms they forced Him to kneel his battered body to the ground as they tied the patibulum beam across His bloody lacerated shoulders like the other two prisoners. Once the patibulum beam was secured to His body then His naked body was pushed over backwards as the two soldiers yanked on the ropes around His forearms. This action caused His blood stained head wearing the crown of three inch woven thorns to hit the rocky hill with a thud. The two soldiers with the ropes continued to stretch His arms as they lined up His wrists with the pre-drilled holes in the wooden patibulum beam. Next, while the soldiers held His arms stretched tight to where His shoulders were almost pulled out of the sockets, a soldier with a heavy hammer placed the pin sharp tapered end of a nine-inch steel stake on the top of His wrist lining it up with the pre-drilled hole. The soldier then raised the steel mallet into the air and smacked the steel stake on the head driving the spike through the flesh of the wrist of the Messiah crushing the ulna nerve and sending a stream of red blood into the air like a fountain. He continued to drive the steel spike through the flesh of the Messiah until the flat wooden piece at the top of the spike was tight against the flesh of the wrist of the Messiah. The flat wooden piece kept the victims from trying to dislodge the spikes from their tied arms. The same process took place on the other wrist of Yahusha once again sending a fountain of blood spurting into the air when the spike tore through the flesh of the wrist of the Messiah. Then the Messiah was rolled over face first into the dirt landing with a jolting thud so that the soldier with the steel mallet could bend over the tapered end of the steel spikes on the backside of the wooden patibulum beam. Once the spikes were bent over the Messiah was rolled back over once again as His body was violently thrown over as a soldier held on to His legs.

Long ropes were thrown over the cross of the vertical pole and tied to the steel rings that were attached to the patibulum. Then the battered and bloody body of the Messiah was hoisted up the vertical pole as part of His lacerated flesh of His lower back, buttocks and backs of His legs scrapped up the rough vertical pole like sandpaper that tore any loose flesh from His body. Once He was at the crossbeam of the pole the patibulum was secured to the crossbeam and the ropes that were used to pull Him up were loosened and detached from the steel rings. Next, the soldier with the steel mallet took another long steel spike while a soldier held the leg of the Messiah against the side of the vertical pole and drove the spike though the ankle of the Messiah attaching it to the pole. Then the process was repeated to the other ankle on the opposite side of the pole. This was predicted in the Scriptures of the Holy Writ in the book of *Thillahyim* (Psalms) chapter twenty-two verses fifteen through seventeen, **"Like waters I am spilled forth and all My bones are spread out My heart is like wax It is melted to liquid in the center of My intestines. My strength is dried up like a piece of pottery and My tongue clings to My jaws. To the powdered grey clay dust of death You have hung Me because yelping dogs have surrounded Me. A tight band of those who do moral evil have surrounded Me. They bore open by piercing My hands and My feet."**

Once the Messiah had been impaled on the cross of capital punishment, which was now shortly after the third hour (nine 'clock a.m.), the Roman soldiers distributed the Messiah's clothes by throwing bits of wood to see who would get what especially His one piece tunic and then sitting down they guarded Him there. First the Roman warriors took His dress and made four sections out of it giving each warrior a section. Then they took His tunic shirt which was a single piece knitted from the top throughout and they said to one another, "Let us not split it but let us cast lots." Therefore, the Scriptures of the Holy Writ could verify the prediction which said in *Thillahyim* (Psalms) chapter twenty-two verse eighteen, **"They split and distribute My clothing among them and for My garment they made fall a lot."** The captain allowed close family members and devoted followers of Yahusha to position themselves in front of the crowd about five yards away from the foot of the cross. In that group was *Shim'own* (Simon) who had lost his two young sons in the angry crowd and had carried the patibulum for the Messiah to Calvary. In front of *Shim'own* (Simon) near the cross of capital punishment stood the mother of Yahusha, *Miryam* (Mary) and her sister *Shalowmit* (Salome) who stood to her right. On the left hand of *Miryam* (Mary) the mother of Yahusha stood *Miryam* (Mary) of *Migdal* (Magdalene) and to the right of *Shalowmit* (Salome) stood her son *Yowchanan* (John) the young cousin of Yahusha, whom He loved. On the right of *Yowchanan* (John) stood *Miryam* (Mary) the wife of *Ach'ab* (Alphaeus).

Yahusha struggled to catch His breath as He pushed up on the spikes through His ankles sending excruciating pain up His legs said in an slow exhausted and airy voice as He looked towards the heavens with His nearly swollen shut black and blue eyes and pleaded, "Father take away this sin from them because they do not know what they are doing." Then the soldiers placed an inscription engraved on a wooden titled placard above His head His alleged crime having been ordered by *Pilatos*, "THIS IS YAHUSHA NAZARETH THE SOVEREIGN OF THE YHUDIY." When some of the *kohen* (priests) saw the wooden title placard they sent some of their legal scribes (lawyers) scurrying to the palace of *Pilatos* (Pilate) to complain. They expressed with great passion to *Pilatos*, "Do not write, '*the Sovereign of the Yhudiy*' but that He said '*I Exist*

33

as the Sovereign of the Yhudiy'!" Pilatos was angered that they would come to him with such hatred and envy for Yahusha that he quipped in response to their whining request, "What I have written, I have written!" Then he had them ushered out of his presence. Certainly, many of the Yhudiy (Jews) read to know again this title placard because the location where Yahusha was impaled on the cross was so close to Yruwshalaim (Jerusalem) the Great City. It was written in *Hebraisti* (Aramaic), *Hellenisi* (Greek) and *Rhomaisti* (Latin). Also, at that time, two brigand thieves were impaled on crosses with Him, one off to the right and one off to the left.

Some of the curious onlookers traveled near Him and spoke impiously vilifying Him and shaking their heads, wagging their tongues and laying forth profane words, "Aha! You Who was going to demolish the Temple and in three days construct it, save Yourself, if you are the Son of Yahuah! And descend down from the cross for capital punishment!" Similarly, also the high priests were jeering at and deriding Him with the scribes and the senior members of the Sanhedrin, laying forth words, "He saved different ones but He is not able to save Himself! He is Sovereign of Yisra'Yah (Israel). Let him descend down now from the cross of capital punishment and we will have faith in and entrust our spiritual well-being to Him, the Messiah!" Others jeered, "He is convinced to rely on Yahuah, let Him rush and rescue Him now, if He desires Him since He is the Favorite One of Yahuah! For this reason, He said, 'I Exist as the Son of Yahuah!" Also one of the brigands that were impaled in the company with Him did the same and defamed, railed at, chided and taunted Him. The brigand thief on the left shouted, "If You are the Messiah save Yourself and us!" However, the crucified thief on the right responded and admonished the other criminal saying, "Do you not fear Yahuah since you are in the same decision for your crime?

In fact, we are equitable and deserve what we received for the things that we have done, but this One has done not one thing out-of-place, injurious or wicked," Then the one on the right looked at Yahusha and expressed, "Bear me in mind and recollect me Master when You come into Your royalty, realm and rule." Yahusha with love and compassion replied, "Firmly, I relate to you in words that on this day you will be with Me in Paradise, the park of future happiness." These actions and words were also predicted in the Scriptures of the Holy Writ in the book of *Thillahyim* (Psalms) chapter twenty-two and verses seven and eight, **"But I am a maggot and not a man and the disgrace of men and diseteemed by the people. All who see Me deride and laugh at Me and they stick out and emit their lips and they waver back and forth the head."**

Now it had been nearly three long hours since the crucifixion had taken place. Yahusha loudly gasping for air slightly lifted His blood stained and thorn encircled head and looked down to speak to His mother *Miryam* (Mary). As salty tears continued to stream down her soft cheeks and her lips quivered as she bemoaned her shattered and broken heart, Yahusha could see His mother in deep grief and the pupil whom He loved, cousin *Yowchanan* (John) now standing beside her since her strength to remain standing waned. With much effort and a half broken voice Yahusha *HaMachiach* (the Messiah) with deep compassion expressed to His mother, "Woman, lo your son." Then He looked at *Yowchanan* (John) and a trail of dirt went from his eyes down to the hairs on his young beard caused by the constant flow of painful tears and the dust in the air. Yahusha in a loud whispering and broken voice said to His cousin, "Lo, your mother." It was from that hour that *Yowchanan* (John) took *Miryam* (Mary) into his own home.

Shim'own (Simon) who had been standing there for what had seemed like years losing all sense of time, suddenly felt two small soft hands tightly grab each of his from behind. As he looked down the two small boys were standing there frightened, confused and weeping with small tears streaming down their small innocent cheeks. Then he heard the oldest one, *Alexandros* (Alexander) say through his small quivering voice, "Father, please forgive us, the lamb got loose and ran away." Through the tears he continued, *"Ab, Ab (*Father, father) what happened here today? We are so scared and we don't understand." So *Shim'own* (Simon) picked up his two sobbing boys, held them tightly on each of his hips and turned them towards the cross. As tears of joy and strong compassion and deep love for the Messiah Yahusha filled his eyes he said to his two sobbing small boys as they clung tightly to his shoulders, "My sweet boys look there is the Lamb."

4

Shortly beginning the six hour (twelve o'clock noon) the Vulture of Death shrieked with an eerie tone and it left the Temple pinnacle and began to hover in a circle over the hill called *Gulgoleth* (Golgotha). In unison pitch black clouds began to rapidly cover the sun and fill the sky over the Great City of Yruwshalaim (Jerusalem). The wind began to pick up and plumes of dust began to fill the air. Then darkness came into being over all the soil of the globe that lasted until the ninth hour (three o'clock p.m.). The air turned very cool and the wind began to gust without prevail. Deep rumblings of muffled thunder could now be heard in a not-so-far-off distance. The soldiers grew nervous and many in the crowd were sent scurrying back inside the wall of Yruwshalaim (Jerusalem) seeking safety from what seemed to be a violent storm brewing. Those left in the crowd were a few of the legal scribes (lawyers) of the Sanhedrin, four Temple guards assigned for the safety of the scribes and a handful of unscrupulous men hired by the *Parash* (Pharisees) to be a witness to the very end of this heinous and unlawful crime committed by the *HaGadowl Kohen* (The Chief High Priest). Also near the foot of the cross of capital punishment were the mother of Yahusha, *Miryam* (Mary) and her sister *Shalowmit* (Salome) and her son *Yowchanan* (John), *Miryam* (Mary) of *Migdal* (Magdalene) and finally *Miryam* (Mary) the wife of *Ach'ab* (Alphaeus).

About the ninth hour (three o'clock in the afternoon) Yahusha exclaimed for an invitation in a loud tone relating in words in the Hebrew language, "Yah, Yah, 'azab" or translated in the Greek language, "Eli, Eli, lama sabachthani!" That is translated as "My Yahuah, my Yahuah why did You let Me remain?" The Messiah was quoting King David who had predicted and written nearly one-thousand years earlier in the book of *Thillahyim* (Psalms) chapter twenty-two and verse one that this would be said at the crucifixion of the coming Messiah, "**Yahuah, My Yah why have You relinquished Me and is My Yahusha at a remote place of time, the spoken words of the matter of My sighing?**" Instantly, some of those standing there heard this and related in words, "This One addresses by name, *Yisha'Yah* (Elijah)!" Then at once one of them ran and took a sponge, filled it with sour wine vinegar and put it on a reed and furnished Yahusha a drink. However, the remaining ones bitterly laid forth words, "Go away! Let us see if *Yisha'Yah* (Elijah) is coming to save and deliver Him!" Yahusha once more exclaimed with a loud tone saying, "Father, into the power of Your hands I deposit and place alongside You My breath. It has been completed!" Then Yahusha slanted His head and surrendered the vitality of the breath of His spirit. At once, the curtain screen to the Most Holy Place of the Temple was split into two pieces from above until downwards. Then the soil of the whole globe rocked with vibration and thrown into tremors and the mass of rocks were split. Also the remembrance tombs in the city of Yruwshalaim (Jerusalem) of people who were actually buried elsewhere were opened up and many bodies of the deceased blameless were roused from death. However, they did not enter into the sacred city until after the resurgence of death by Yahusha which then at that time were exhibited to many. The captain of one hundred men and those with him who were guarding Yahusha, upon seeing the gale of air and the earthquake of the ground and the many things that came into being, were frightened in a high degree. The Roman captain related in words, "Truly this One was the Son of Yahuah, innocent in character and holy in actions!" All the throng of rabble who had appeared together being spectators of this spectacle and had remained to the end, looked intensely at the things that had just came into being and they beat their chests repeatedly with their hands and returned home.

Accordingly, the Yhudiy (Jews) leaders since it was the Day of Readiness before *Pecach* (Passover) they did not want the bodies to stay on the cross of capital punishment for exposure to death on the *Shabbath* (Sabbath holiday, day of rest) since it was a special *Shabbath* day. Therefore they requested of Pilatos to break to pieces and crack apart their legs and then be taken away after they died. The Roman captain of one hundred men gave the orders to break their legs so a Roman soldier with a big wooden club came up to the first thief on the cross and with all his might swung three times and struck the shin bones of his legs and broke them to pieces and cracked apart the legs until the bloody bones were protruding through the flesh of the victim. Then he came up to the thief on the right of Yahusha who was impaled in the company with Him and repeated his actions. But when he came up to Yahusha he saw that He was even now dead, thus he did not rend to pieces and crack apart His legs. Therefore, one of the Roman warriors took his lance and nudged with a heavy prick His side below the ribs and at once blood and water issued forth. Young Yowchanan (John) later was a witness to this as the truth. He was unaware of it at this time but later he would be required to testify as a witness that his testimony given was true and that one known as Yowchanan (John) knows that he does speak the truth in order that others may have faith to entrust their spiritual well-being to the Messiah.

For this reason, those things came into being in order that the Scriptures of the Holy Writ could verify the prediction in *Thillah*

(Psalm) chapter thirty-four verse twenty, *"Putting a hedge of thorns about to guard and protect all His bones. Not one of them is tossed in a violent or sudden manner."* Once more a different Scripture of the Holy Writ expresses in the book of *Zkaryah* (Zechariah) chapter twelve verses ten and eleven, *"I will pour upon the house of David and upon the dwellers of the city of Yruwshalaim (Jerusalem) the Breath of grace and earnest prayers. They will look intently at with pleasure upon Me whom they have pierced and they will weep and bemoan for Him as one tears at the hair and beats the breasts in grief for an only son and will be bitter over Him like the bitterness over the death of the firstborn. On that day of sunset to sunset will be great lamenting in the city of Yruwshalaim (Jerusalem) like the lamentation of the city of Hadadrimmown in the Valley of Mgiddown* **(Hadadrimmon in the valley of Megiddo)."**

Early evening came into being before sunset to end the day of Wednesday and a human being abounding with great wealth came from Ramah (Arimathea) by the name of Yowceph (Joseph) and was known as Yowceph from the Estates of Arimathea. Yowceph was noble in rank and was a member and adviser of the Sanhedrin. However, being of high rank on the Sanhedrin he refused to be in the company with the Messiah's accusers on the Council and would not deposit his vote with their practice and purpose. Not only was he a pupil of Yahusha *HaMachiach* (The Messiah) he was the uncle of the mother of Yahusha, Miryam (Mary) who was called by family members as he was growing up, *Qatan Yow* (Little Joe). The wealthy great-uncle of the Messiah approached and came near to Pilatos and asked for the body of Yahusha. Pilatos was struck with admiration that He had already died. So, having summoned and called to himself the captain of one hundred men who had been in charge of guarding Yahusha at the Place of the Skull, he inquired of him how long He had been dead. After Pilatos knew the facts from the captain of one hundred soldiers he bestowed gratuitously the body of Yahusha to Yowceph. Therefore, at that time Pilatos ordered it to be given to him.

Then Yowceph went to the market and purchased a new bleached linen cloth. After leaving the market, which was shutting down because sunset was quickly approaching, Yowceph went to the Place of the Skull where the lifeless battered body of Yahusha hung on that wooden cross. The wind was still blowing hard and it was raining tears of grief from the dark and rolling black clouds above. After the body was lowered down from the cross, Yowceph took possession of the body and twisted and entwined it in strips of the clean bleached linen cloth and placed it in his own tomb which he had quarried in the mass of rock. Since it was nearing sunset, he blocked against the door of the entrance a large stone and he departed to prepare for *Pecach* (Passover). Miryam of Migdal (Mary Magdalene) and Miryam (Mary) the mother of Ya'aqob, the small one (James the Lesser) and Yowceph (Joses) were spectators to know where He had been placed. They had sit down in front of the tomb until Yowceph of Arimathea had the stone rolled in front of the entrance. Then they departed following him back to the Great City and observed *Pecach* (Passover) from sundown on Wednesday to sunset on Thursday.

On the next day, following Pecach (Passover), Friday morning which is after the readiness, the *Koehn* (high priests) were convened together with the *Parash* (Pharisees) and they went to see Pilatos. Pilatos was in no mood to listen to their quibbling and whining but he knew that he had to keep peace in Yruwshalaim (Jerusalem) at all costs. Therefore he ordered the armed guards who were standing at the Great Hall doors to allow them to present themselves in front of his throne. After they bowed their heads in respect to him, Pilatos said, "What do you want now? I already gave you everything you wanted in regards to that man called Yahusha!" Then one of the *Kohen* (high priests) related in words, "Sir, we have recollected that that imposter and roving tramp said while He was still living, *'After three days I will rouse from death."* The *koehn* (high priest) continued, "Order then the grave to be rendered secure until the third day, lest His pupils come by night and filch Him and say to the people, *'He is roused from death!"* and the last will be more evil and aggravated than the first." Pilatos being short on patience with the Hebrew religious elite snipped, "You possess a Roman sentry! Withdraw and render secure as you know how!" Then the religious elite traveled and rendered secure the grave, stamping for security with the private mark the stone, with the Roman sentry. Being satisfied with the Roman sentry standing guard, the *koehn* (high priests) scurried to their own homes to prepare for the regular *Shabbath* (Sabbath, Friday sunset to Saturday Sunset).

While the evil Hebrew religious elite were committing their sinister deeds and doing the work of Satan Friday morning and afternoon and the day after the special *Shabbath* (Sabbath) of *Pecach* (Passover) from Wednesday sunset to Thursday sunset meanwhile elapsed, Miryam (Mary) of Migdal, Miryam (Mary) the mother of Ya'aqob (James) the lessor and *Shalowmit* (Salome) the mother of Ya'kov (James) and his brother Yowchanan (John) who was also the sister of Miryam (Mary) the mother of the Messiah Yahusha, went to the market to purchase aromatic spices in order that that they would go to the tomb after the regular *Shabbath* (Sabbath) and anoint the body of the Messiah with perfumed oil. After their purchase of the aromatic spices they went back to join the others to prepare the perfumed oil and to get ready for the regular *Shabbath* (Sabbath) beginning at sundown. For this reason they refrained from labor on the regular *Shabbath* (Sabbath) according to the authoritative injunction of the Hebrew Law.

At the close of the day of the regular *Shabbath* (Sabbath) very early Sunday morning at the daybreak of dawn as it began to grow light into the first day of the week, came Miryam (Mary) of Migdal and the different Miryam (Mary) with the aromatic scents of the spices and perfumed oil which they had prepared to discern the grave of the Messiah. Some other people were with them also. By the time they had reached the tomb of the Messiah the sun had already risen. On the way there, they related in words to themselves, "Who will roll away the stone from the door of the tomb for us?" Lo! A gale of air and a great earthquake of the ground came into being because a messenger angel bringing tidings from Yahuah descended down from heaven, the eternal abode of Yahuah and approaching and coming near rolled away the stone and sat down on it. The sight of him was in the manner of the glare of lightning and his apparel was white as descending snow. From the fright of him, the Roman sentries who were guarding to keep an eye upon the tomb, were rocked and thrown into a tremor and they became as if dead. The women looked up and saw that the stone had been rolled away. For this reason the women became perplexed, the stone was very big. At the sight of the open tomb, Miryam (Mary) of Migdal ran hastily and came to Shim'own Kepha (Simon Peter) and to the different pupil whom loved Yahusha. Being out of breath with panting and sobbing she laid forth words, "They have taken away the Messiah out of the burial place and we do not know where they placed Him."

The rest of the women entered into the opened tomb and did not find the body of Messiah Yahusha. It came into their perplexity about this and instead saw two youth under forty years-old sitting on the right with the clothing of a white long-fitting gown that flashed like lightning and they were utterly astonished. When they became alarmed and filled with fear and reclined their faces to the soil, one of the angels responded and said to the women, "You do not be alarmed because I know that you are seeking Yahusha the *Nazarenos*, the One having been impaled on the cross. He is not in this spot! For this reason, He has wakened and roused from death as he said. Come here and see the spot where He was outstretched. Now exercise your mind and remember how He uttered in words to you while you were still in *Galiylah* (Galilee). He related in those words that it was necessary for the Son of Man to be yielded up into the hands of sinful human beings and to be impaled on the cross and on the third day stand up again." Then the women recollected His utterance on this topic and the angel continued, "Travel without delay to speak to His pupils and to *Kepha* (Peter) that He has wakened and roused from death and lo, He precedes you into *Galiylah* (Galilee). There you will gaze at Him with wide opened eyes. Lo! I have spoken to you." The women issued out suddenly without delay from the remembrance grave and they ran away from the tomb. They were gripped with the quaking fear and the bewilderment of ecstasy. They told no one on the way back to the pupils anything because they were in awe and frightened.

In the meantime as the women were on their way back to the city of Yruwshalaim (Jerusalem), Shim'own Kepha (Simon Peter), Yowchanan (John) and Miryam (Mary) of Migdal issued out and ran to the burial place. The two men ran hastily to the same place at the same place of time but Yowchanan (John) ran forward more swiftly and speedily than Kepha (Peter) and came first to the burial place. Yowchanan leaned over and peered within and looked at the linen bandages laying outstretched. However, he did not enter the tomb. Certainly, Shim'own Kepha (Simon Peter) who had accompanied him entered into the place of burial and he was a spectator of the linen bandages lying outstretched. The towel that was used to bind the face of the corpse of Yahusha which was on His head was not lying outstretched with the linen bandages but was in a separate space being entwined into one spot. Accordingly, at that time Yowchanan (John) also entered and was the one who had come to the burial spot first and he saw and had faith to entrust his spiritual well-being to the Messiah. For this reason, they did not know yet the Scripture of the Holy Writ that it was necessary for Him to stand up from being a dead corpse. Then the pupils departed to themselves once more.

However, Miryam (Mary) of Migdal remained behind and stood at the burial spot sobbing and wailing out loud. Then she leaned over to peer within the burial place and was a spectator of two messenger angels in white sitting down with one at the head and one at the feet where the body of Yahusha had lain outstretched. They expressed to her, "Woman why do you sob and wail out loud?" She related in words and replied to them, "Because they took away my Messiah and I do not know where they placed Him." After these words she twisted around to the back and was a spectator of Yahusha standing but she did not know that it was Yahshua. Yahshua related in words to her, "Woman why do you sob and wail out loud? Whom do you seek?" Miryam (Mary) thought it was the garden keeper so she expressed to Him, "Sir, if You have lifted and carried Him away speak to me where you placed Him, and I will take Him away." Yahshua related in words to her, "Miryam (Mary)!" Miryam (Mary) who had twisted around expressed to Him, "Rhabboni!" In Hebrew this is said to express Instructor. Yahusha related in words to her, "Do not touch me because I have not gone up to the Father. Instead travel to My brothers and tell them that I am going up to My Father and your Father and My Yahuah and your Yahuah." Thus the Messiah having stood up at the daybreak of dawn on the first day of the week first showed the light of Himself to Miryam (Mary) of Migdal from whom He had ejected seven demonic beings. Just before it got dark, Miryam (Mary) of Midgal came back to the pupils who were grieving and sobbing out loud from the news of Kepha (Peter) and Yowchanan (John). She announced to the pupils that she had stared at the Anointed Messiah and He spoke to her these things. However, those who heard that He lives looked closely at her and they disbelieved.

As Miryam (Mary) of Migdal was on her way back to the pupils so was Miryam (Mary) the mother of Ya'aqob (James) the lessor and *Shalowmit* (Salome) the mother of Ya'kov (James) and his brother Yowchanan (John) who instead of taking all the dangerous shortcuts had taken the safer long way back and they ran into some of the Roman sentry who were returning to the city and they hid until it was safe which delayed their return. They were full of fear and great cheerfulness and ran hastily when they could to announce the words of the angels to the pupils of the Messiah. Also, lo, on the way of return Yahusha encountered them relating in words, "Be well!" They came near and seized His feet and prostrated themselves to Him in homage, reverence and adoration. Then Yahusha related in words to them, "Do not be frightened! Withdraw to announce to My brothers that they may go off to Galiylah (Galilee) and in that place they will see Me." They returned from the place of burial and announced all these things to all eleven ambassadors of the Gospel and being official commissioners of the Messiah and to all the remaining ones. However, they too were met with disbelief and their words were received as nonsense.

Also, while all the women were on their way back to the pupils, some of the Roman sentry were coming into the city and announced to the *Kohen* (high priests) all the things that had come into being. So the *Kohen* (high priests) convened together with the senior members of the Sanhedrin and took advisement from a deliberative body and gave ample enough silver cash to the warriors. The Sanhedrin told the Roman warriors, "Say that His pupils came by night and filched Him while we were put to sleep. If this is heard in front of the chief of the province, Pilatos, we will convince him and we will make you free from being anxious." Therefore, the Roman warriors took the silver cash and did as they were taught. This thing said by them was reported thoroughly and divulged by the Yhudiy (Hebrews) even until today.

Later that afternoon as the others were debating what had been told to them, Kepha (Peter) tossed and turned in his mind and could not make sense of it as he pondered upon the words spoken by Miryam (Mary) of Migdal and then the other women. Their words echoed over and over with the loudness of a shofar horn, yet how could their words be true. The longer he pondered them, the louder their words rang in his head and the harder he tossed and turned inside his mind and he began to sweat profusely. Finally, he got up from his mat and went outside into the cool air to help clear his troubled mind and disbelieving heart. The afternoon streets were very still and quiet with an occasional dog barking deep within the city. He closed his eyes and rubbed them with his big fists to clear the sleepy matter from them. When he opened them he saw the figure of a man not far from him in the street. This startled Kepha (Peter) and he barked, "Who goes there? Identify yourself!" A voice came from the figure and said, "Kepha (Peter) how many times must you deny Me, your Messiah and disbelieve before the cock crows tomorrow morning? The words sent to you are true."

Yahusha the risen Messiah continued, "You heard Me tell the Pharisees that the only supernatural sign that they would get was the supernatural sign of the inspired prophet Yonah (Jonah). For exactly like Yonah (Jonah) was in the abdomen cavity of the huge fish for three days and three nights, in the same way the Son of Man would be in the heart of the soil for three days and three nights. Therefore I descended down into the interior parts of Hades. While there I heralded as a public crier and announced the divine truth and good news of the Gospel to the spirits of dead corpses in the guarded place in order that they would not be judicially tried, condemned and punished indeed according to human beings in the flesh but could live according to Yahuah in the Sacred Breath (Holy Spirit). These were the willful and perverse disbelieving ones when one time failed the patience of Yahuah in the day of Noach (Noah) when he constructed the box and saved the eight breaths of spirt of his family and was protected from the down pouring of rain water. I also grabbed and now possess for eternity the keys of Death and Hades. Then on the third day I arose from death and returned from the depths of Hades victorious as King David predicted in **Thillah (Psalm) chapter sixteen and verse ten, 'Because You will not relinquish My vitality of breath to Sh'owl (Hades) the world of the dead. You will not give Your Sacred One to see corruption.'** I told you that I must suffer the death of a cross and then I would rise on the third day."

Then Yahusha the Messiah revealed His face and Kepha (Peter) fell face first to the ground and exclaimed as he began to weep, "My Lord!" He felt Yahusha touch the top of his head so he slowly raised his head and tearful eyes to look up and before him was the nail scared hand of the Messiah reaching to help him to his feet. Kepha (Peter) quickly ran inside to inform the others who were still debating what the women had told them. However, when they reached the gate there was no one and nothing in sight to greet them except the empty street and stillness of the afternoon. Thus Kepha (Peter) was the third appearance of the Messiah Yahusha after He had risen from the cold darkness of death.

5

After these things that same late afternoon, two men that had been pupils of the Messiah were walking at large and were going to a little village named Emmaous, meaning 'warm springs', which was about seven miles from the Great City of Yruwshalaim (Jerusalem). They conversed with one another about all these things that transpired. Then it came to be as they were conversing and discussing even Yahusha Himself approached near and joined together with them as they were traveling into the field of the country farm. Yahusha rendered Himself apparent in a different shape and nature and their eyes were seized so as not to become fully acquainted with Him. Yahusha inquired of them, "What was this that you were saying that you exchanged with one another while you were walking and treading about and now are gloomy with a mournful appearance?" One of the men responded whose name was Kleopas and said to Him, "Are you merely a foreigner in Yruwshalaim (Jerusalem) and do not know the things that have come into being during these days?" Yahusha questioned them further, "What things?"

Kleopas shook his head in frustration and amazement and answered Yahusha *HaMachiach* (the Messiah), "The things about Yahusha of Nazareth, who was a man, an inspired prophet, powerful in actions and what He said in the presence of Yahuah and all the people. How both the *Kohen* (High Priests) and our first in rank and power yielded Him up to the decision of death and impaled Him on the cross. But we were expecting Him to be the One about to ransom *Yisra'Yah* (Israel). But with all these things, this third day is present today since these things came into being. Also, some women from us put us out of our wits and we have become astounded being at dawn, up at daybreak at the place of burial. They did not find His body and came relating in words that they saw in a vision of angels bringing tidings who expressed in speech that He was alive. Some of those with us departed to the place of burial and found in the same way also, just as the women had said. But they did not see Him."

Yahusha sighed and said, "Oh unintelligent ones and slow in heart of feelings and thoughts to trust your spiritual well-being to *HaMachiach* (the Messiah) on all things which the inspired prophets talked about! Was it not necessary for *HaMachiach* (the Messiah) to experience the sensation of pain for these things and enter into His glory?" Then Yahusha commencing from Mosheh (Moses) and from all the inspired prophets, He explained thoroughly and translated to them in all the Scriptures of the Holy Writ that was about Himself. They approached near to the village where they were traveling and He pretended to be traveling on to a greater distance. They compelled Him relating in words, "Stay with us because it is towards evening and the day has reclined." So He entered to stay with them. It came to be as He was reclining down at His place at the table with them, He took a raised loaf of bread and blessed it with a benediction and broke the bread and gave it to them. Then their eyes were opened thoroughly and they became fully acquainted with Him. Then He became invisible to them. They said to one another, "Was not our heart of feelings and thoughts kindled with fire in us as He talked to us on the road and as He expounded the Scriptures of the Holy Writ?"

Standing up in that same hour, they departed and returned to Yruwshalaim (Jerusalem). Then being nightfall on that day, the first day of the week the doors had been closed where the pupils were convened together because they were frightened of the Yhuwdiy (Hebrew) leaders. They found the ten convened together and the remaining ones with them. Then they announced by relating in words as a set discourse, "The Master really has roused from laying in death and was seen with wide open eyes by Shim'own Kepha (Simon Peter)!" Then they unfolded the things to the remaining ones the things that happened on the road and how He became known to them during the fracturing of the loaf of raised bread. However, the nine did not believe them either. Eventually as all were reclining at a meal that evening, He was rendered apparent to the ten and He railed at them because of their disbelief and unfaithfulness of disobedience and their hard-heartedness because they did not believe those who looked closely at Him having been roused from the lying down of death.

Thus when the two men who had been on the road to Emmaous who were still relating all these things to them with their announcement and the nine with some of the others who remained began ridiculing them with disbelief, Yahusha Himself stood in the middle of them and related in words to them with disbelief, "Shalom! (Peace to you!)" But being scared like birds flying away and being filled with fear, they thought they were spectators of a spirit. He said to them, "Why are you agitated and why do these discussions go up in your hearts of feeling and thoughts? See My hands, My feet and My side, I EXIST as Him! Manipulate Me and see because a spirit does not have flesh and bones as you are a spectator of Me possessing." After having said this, He exhibited to them the hands and the feet. They were still disbelieving from the cheerfulness and delight and admiration. Yet certainly the pupils were cheerful and happy seeing the Messiah.

Therefore, Yahusha said to them, "Do you possess anything to eat here?" They gave Him a share of the roasted fish. He took it and ate it in front of them. Then He said, "These are the words that I uttered to you while I was with you, that the thing written in the Law of Mosheh (Moses) and in the inspired prophets and in the Thillahyim (Psalms) are necessary to verify their predictions about Me." Then He opened thoroughly their minds to comprehend the Scriptures of the Holy Writ. He continued teaching them in words, "Thus it was written: It is necessary that the Messiah experience the divine truth of the Gospel on the authority and character of His name for a reversal of a decision and compunction for reformation and the pardon and freedom of sins to all the foreign nations, commencing from Yruwshalaim (Jerusalem). You are witnesses of these things. Lo! I am sending you out on a mission with the announcement as a pledge of divine assurance of My Father upon you. I say to you once more, *Shalom* (Pease to you)! Just as the Father has sent Me out on a Mission, I also dispatch you. But you sit down and dwell in the Great City of Yruwshalaim (Jerusalem) until which time you are invested in the clothing of the miraculous power from the elevated sky." After saying this He blew a puff on them and related in words to them, "Take and get a hold of the Sacred Breath (Holy Spirit)! Whomever you send away their sins, they have been sent away from them. Whomever you retain, they have been retained!"

However, Ta'owm (Thomas) one of the twelve, the one called 'Twin' was not with them when Yahusha came. Certainly, the different pupils related in words to him, "We have seen *HaMachiach* (the Messiah)!" But he said to them, "Unless I see the scar of the spikes in His hands and throw my finger into the scar of the spikes and throw my hand into His side, in no way will I have faith to entrust my spiritual well-being to the Messiah!" After eight days, once more His pupils were inside and Ta'owm (Thomas) was with them. Yahusha came with the doors having been closed and stood in the middle and said, "Shalom (Pease to you)!" Moreover, He related in words to Ta'owm (Thomas), "Bring your finger here in this spot and see My hands and bring your hand and throw it into My side and do not become disbelieving and without faith but trusting!" Ta'owm responded and said to Him, "My *Machiach* (Messiah) and My Yahuah!" Yahusha related I words to Him, "Because you have stared at Me, Ta'owm (Thomas) you possess the faith to entrust your spiritual well-being to the Messiah. Supremely blest are those not seeing yet possessing faith to entrust their spiritual well-being to *HaMachiach* (the Messiah)!" This was the sixth appearance of Yahusha the Messiah after His resurrection from the dead.

Yahusha *HaMachiach* appeared for the seventh time after His resurrection from the dead when the chosen eleven pupils traveled north from the Great City of Yruwshalaim (Jerusalem) to the territory of Galiylah (Galilee) to the mountain where Yahusha had arranged and assigned to them. When they saw Him they prostrated themselves in homage doing reverence and adoration but they wavered in opinion. Yahusha approached and talked with them relating in words as a set discourse, "All privilege and delegated influence in heaven, the eternal abode of Yahuah and upon the soil of the globe has been given to Me. Accordingly, travel into the entire world and herald as a public crier the divine truth and good message of the Gospel to all creation and disciple all the foreign pagan nations. The ones having faith and entrusting their spiritual well-being to *HaMachiach* (the Messiah) shall be saved, delivered and protected. Also submerge them to be fully wet in the baptism of them in the name of the Father Yahuah, and of the Son Yahusha and of the Sacred Breath, teaching them to guard from loss or injury by keeping an eye upon all things, whatever I enjoined you. But he who is unbelieving and disbelieves in disobedience will be sentenced a judgment against him. To those having faith and entrusting their spiritual well-being to *HaMachiach* (the Messiah), these supernatural indications will follow near in the authority and character of My Name, demonic beings will be ejected. They will speak new tongues and languages. They will lift up and take sly and cunning snakes with their hands and if they drink anything fatal that is poisonous, not at all will it injure them. They will place hands on the sick and they will possess wellness. Lo! I EXIST with you all the days even until the entire completion of the consummation of the age." Then they all departed down from the mountain.

Even after all these things said and done, Yahusha appeared for the eighth time after His resurrection from the dead. Yahusha rendered Himself apparent again to some of His pupils on the Sea of Tiberias. In this way He rendered Himself apparent. Shim'own Kepha (Simon Perter) the big fisherman, and Ta'owm (Thomas) being called Twin and Nthane'l (Nathanel) from Qanah (Cana) of the territory of Galiylah (Galilee) and the two sons of Zabdiy the first cousins of Yahusha, Ya'kov (James) and Yowchanan (John) and two different ones of His followers. Shim'own Kepha (Simon Peter) expressed to them, "I am withdrawing to fish." They related to him in words, "We are also coming with you." So they issued out and went up into the sailing vessel. During that night they captured not even one fish. But even now it was becoming dawn and Yahusha stood on the beach where the waves dashed. However, the pupils did not know it was Yahusha. Certainly Yahusha related in words to them, "Children, don't you have anything to eat?" They responded to Him, "No". He said to them, "Throw the fishing seine to the right side of the sailing vessel and you will find." Accordingly, they threw it and they did not have enough force to drag it because of the large number of fish. Then Yowchanan (John), the Messiah's young cousin whom Yahusha loved expressed to Kepha (Peter), "It is *HaMachiach* (the Messiah)!"

Certainly, Shim'own Kepha (Simon Peter) heard that it was *HaMachiach* (the Messiah) and girded tightly his outer garment for he was nude and threw himself into the sea. The different pupils came in the boat because they were not a great distance from the soil of the beach, only about two-hundred cubits (one hundred yards) and were trailing the fishing seine of fish. Certainly, when they disembarked on the soil of the beach they looked at the bed of burning coals lying outstretched and a fish resting upon them and raised loaves of bread. Yahusha expressed to them, "Bring from the fish which you just now have captured." Shim'own Kepha (Simon Peter) went up and dragged the fishing seine onto the soil of the beach, full of large fish numbering one-hundred and fifty-three. Even being such a vast number the fishing seine was not split. Yahusha related in words to them, "Come here and have breakfast, the principle meal!" Not even one of the pupils had the courage to interrogate Him by saying 'Who are You?' because they knew it was *HaMachiach* (the Messiah). Then Yahusha came and took the raised loaf of bread and gave it to them and similarly the fish. Even now this was the third time Yahusha rendered Himself apparent to Ta'owm (Thomas) after being aroused from lying in death.

Accordingly, when they had breakfast, the principle meal, Yahusha related in words to Shim'own Kepha (Simon Peter), "Shim'own bar Yowchanan (Simon son of John), do you love Me more than these?" Kepha (Peter) expressed to Him, "Yes, Master You know that I am Your friend." Yahusha commanded in response, "Graze My baby lambs." Then Yahusha said a second time, "Shim'own of Yowchanan

(Simon son of John), Do you love Me." He expressed to Him, "You know that I am your friend." Yahusha said to him, "Tend as a shepherd My sheep!" Then He related in words a third time to Kepha (Peter), "Shim'own bar Yowchanan (Simon son of John), are you My friend?" Kepha (Peter) was distressed and sad that He said to him the third time 'Are you My friend?' So he said to Yahusha, "Master, You see and know all things. You know that I am Your friend!" Yahusha related in words to him, "Graze My sheep!"

Yahusha continued to converse with Kepha (Peter), "Firmly and surely, I relate to you in words as a set discourse, when you were youthful you bound about with a belt clothing for yourself and you treaded all around and walked at large where you wished but when you begin to grow old you will extend out your hands and a different one will bind about with a belt clothing for you and will carry you where you do not wish." He said this to indicate by what death he would render glorious Yahuah. After He said this, He related in words to him, "Unite on the road to be in the same way with to accompany Me as a disciple." Kepha (Peter) reverted and saw Yowchanan (John) the pupil whom Yahusha loved, who had leaned back on His chest at the supper being the chief meal in the evening, the night of the betrayal and had asked 'Master who is the one yielding You up!' Yowchanan (John) was on the road to be in the same way with to accompany Him as a disciple. Kepha (Peter) saw this one and expressed to Yahusha, "Master, what about this one?" Yahusha related in words to him, "If I wish for him to stay until I come, what is that to you? You unite on the road to be in the same way with to accompany Me as a disciple!" Accordingly, the reasoning of this thing said issued out to the brothers that that pupil would not die off. However, Yahusha did not say that he would not die off but instead, "If I wish for him to stay until I come what is that to you?"

Yowchanan (John) the younger cousin of Yahusha later became one of the greatest writers of the Scriptures being a witness and testifying with respect to these things as evidence given by him as truth.

Yowceph (Joseph) from the Estates of Arimathea, who claimed the body of Yahusha on the cross and had Him buried in His tomb heard the rumors of the eight appearances of Yahusha. Now Yowceph (Joseph) was noble in rank and was a member and adviser of the Sanhedrin. He was the young uncle of the mother of Yahusha, Miryam (Mary) who was called by family members as he was growing up, *Qatan Yow* (Little Joe). The wealthy great-uncle of Yahusha had amassed his great wealth with mineral contracts with the Roman government and also dealt with the trade routes throughout the middle-east. He was also known amongst the most powerful political circles in Rome itself. He was despised by the *Parash* (Pharisees) and *HaGadowl Kohen* (the Chief High Priest) because of his deep financial ties to the throne of Caesar in Rome and his powerful religious ties in Yruwshalaim (Jerusalem) as an adviser of the Sanhedrin.

Yowceph (Joseph) after pondering on the rumors of the eight appearances of Yahusha decided to invite those who had seen Yahusha to his heavily guarded Estate of Arimathea including his niece, Miryam (Mary) the mother of Yahusha, the eleven pupils, the women who went to the burial place and anyone who had seen Yahusha after His resurrection from the dead. He asked Kepha (Peter) and the others to share their stories with his invited guests who had been carefully selected, making sure the guests did not have any ties to the religious elite in Yruwshalaim (Jerusalem). Over five-hundred guests attended to hear first-hand the stories of Yahusha appearing after His resurrection from death. Yowceph (Joseph) began by explaining to the crowd his relationship with Yahusha as they grew up together. He also explained why He believed that

Yahusha was *HaMachiach* (the Messiah). Then Yowceph called up Kepha (Peter) to represent the eleven and share the four experiences that he had with the appearances of Yahusha since His resurrection. Just as Kepha (Peter) was about to stand in front of the crowd, out of nowhere Yahusha appeared like light. Kepha and those who had been witness to the appearances of Yahusha exclaimed, "My Master!" and immediately dropped their faces to the earth in homage to pay reverence and adoration. Then Yahusha explained to the crowd how He fulfilled the Scriptures of the Holy Writ beginning with Mosheh (Moses) and then through the inspired prophets. This was the ninth appearance of Yahusha after He aroused from lying in death.

On day forty after the resurrection from death by Yahusha He appeared for the tenth and final time to the eleven pupils and those with them. He taught for the last time about the royalty, realm and rule of Yahuah. After convening with them He transmitted a message to them saying, "Do not go away from Yruwshalaim (Jerusalem) but stay around and wait for the announced pledge for the divine assurance of good from the Father which you heard from Me, because Yowchanan Baptista (John the Baptist) submerged to make fully wet in baptism but you will be fully submerged in the baptism of the Sacred Breath (Holy Spirit) after not many of these days." Accordingly, so those convened together inquired of Him, expressing, "Master, at this time are You going to reconstitute the health and organization of the royalty, realm and rule of *Yisra'Yah* (Israel)?" He said to them, "It is not for you to know spaces of time or set and proper times which the Father placed in His own privilege of influence. But you will take and get a hold of miraculous power when the Sacred Breath arrives upon you and you will be witnesses and martyrs of Me in both Yruwshalaim (Jerusalem) and in all the territories of *Yhuwdah* (Judah) and *Shomrown* (Samaria) and to the farthest places of the whole globe." Then Yahusha led them outside as far as *Beythaniy* (Bethany) and having raised up His hands, He blessed them with a benediction.

After saying these things as they were looking at Him, He was raised up and a cloud carried Him upward from their eyes into heaven the eternal abode of Yahuah and sat down at the right side of Yahuah. As they were gazing intently into the sky of His traveling, lo, two men stood beside them in white dress who also said, "Men, *Galiylah'iy* (Galileans) why do you stand looking into the sky? This Yahusha the One being taken up from you into the sky, in this way which He will come like this that you will look closely at Him traveling into the sky." After hearing this news, they prostrated themselves in homage and reverence to Him. At that time they returned to Yruwshalaim (Jerusalem) from the mountain of olive orchards which is near Yruwshalaim (Jerusalem) being a *Shabbath's* (Sabbath's) distance. They were filled with great cheerfulness and delight and were constantly in the Temple all the time praising and blessing Yahuah. After the appointed time of Yahusha, they issued out and heralded as a public crier the divine truth of the Gospel everywhere and the *Machiach* (Messiah) became a co-worker with them and stabilized His Divine Expression through the accompaniment of supernatural indications. Therefore, Yahusha did many different supernatural indications in the front of the faces of His pupils which are not written in the sacred scrolls. But those things have been written in order that you may possess faith to entrust you spiritual well-being to Yahusha *HaMachiach* (the Messiah) the Son of Yahuah and in that possessing faith to entrust your spiritual well-being to *HaMachiach* (the Messiah), you may possess life in His authority and character of His name. Also, there are many things of whatever Yahusha did which if they were all recorded and written down, the world itself could not be a large enough space to write on as a roll.

Also in 30 AD after the ascension of Yahusha to heaven, the eleven pupils did what Yahusha had commanded and stayed in Yruwshalaim (Jerusalem). They along with the women including Miryam (Mary) the mother of Yahusha and His brothers went to the home of the fan maker Ya'kov Gammed Aer (James Walter Ayers). This was the house where Yahusha shared the "Last Supper" with the twelve disciples. When they entered the house they went up to the higher part of the house of the third story apartment where they had been residing permanently while they were in the Great City of Yruwshalaim (Jerusalem). However, before they had gone upstairs to the third story, as soon as little nearly three-year old Yirmyah Achuw Aer (Jerry Lee Ayers) heard the voice of Yowchanan (John) the younger cousin of Yahusha the one that He loved, the little boy ran and leaped into his arms and Yowchanan (John) carried him up the stairs and sat him on his lap. The two of them seemed to be inseparable and the mother of little Yirmyah (Jerry) would have to pry him from Yowchanan (John) when it was bedtime or the disciples needed privacy. However, most of the time Yirmyah (Jerry) would fall asleep in the lap of Yowchanan (John) and he would gently put the sleeping child into his mother's waiting arms. Kepha (Peter) spoke to those gathered because the first order of business was to select a replacement for Yhuwdah Shim'own Iysh'Qriyowth (Judas Simon Iscariot) who had betrayed Yahusha and hung himself in the 'field of blood'. The choice was between two candidates. One was Yowceph (Joseph) called Bar-tsaba meaning "son of army' in the Hebrew language and also called Ioustos (Justus) in the Helen (Greek) language. The other was named Mattihyah (Matthias). They drew lots made from bits of wood and Mattihyah (Matthias) was chosen to be part of the twelve disciples. Ten days after the ascension of Yahusha to heaven was *Chag HaChamishshiym* (Festival of Fifty) which was celebrated for the day Mosheh (Moses) was given the Law on *Har Ciynay* (Mountain Sinai). This festival was to be held fifty days from the *Shabbath* of Friday sunset during *Chag HaMatstsah Lechem* (Festival of Unleavened Bread), Then unexpectedly and suddenly...............

6

...from out of Heaven, the eternal abode of Yahuah, a loud echoing roar as being carried by a violent breeze of a respiration and it filled all the dwelling of the third story apartment belonging to the fan maker Ya'kov Gammed Aer (James Walter Ayers) where the disciples were residing while they were in the Great City of Yruwshalaim (Jerusalem). Then all those present gazed at with wide open eyes being distributed as tongues as if fire like lightning and it settled on each one of them. They were all filled with the Sacred Breath (Holy Spirit) and commenced to talk in different languages as the Sacred Breath gave them to speak.

Even though they were all from *Galiylah* (Galilee) some were speaking in Parthos (Iran), some in Medos (Northwest Iran), some in the language of the Elamites (Southwest Iran), others in the language of those residing permanently in Mesopotamia (Iraq), others in the tongue of those from Kappadokia (Turkey) and Pontos (Northeast Turkey by the Black Sea) even Asia (India), yet different ones in the language of those from Phrugia (West Central Turkey) and Pamphulla (Southwest Turkey), even some the language from Aiuptos (Egypt) and the territories of Libue (Libya Africa) located next to Kurene (Bengasi, Libya), some even the detestable language of the Rhomaios (Romans), while others spoke in the tongue of the people from Kres (Island of Crete) and finally some spoke in the language of those from Araps (Yemen, Oman and Saudi Arabia).

Yhuwdiy (Hebrew) passerby's on the street in front of the lattice work of the windows of third story apartment of the house of the fan maker Ya'kov Gammed Aer (James Walter Ayers) heard the commotion of the different languages and gathered a large crowd. The crowd was put out of their wits and became astounded and were thoroughly puzzled to one another relating in words, "What possibility would you choose this thing to exist?" Some in the gathered crowd threw out their lips and jeered at them expressing, "They are intoxicated with sweet wine made with sugar!"

Then Kepha (Peter) went to the third story window with lattice work and raised his arms and his voice and enunciated plainly to the gathered crowd, "Men, Yhuwdiy (Hebrews) and all those residing in Yruwshalaim (Jerusalem), let this be known to you and listen to take in your ears to my narration on this matter. For this reason it is not in the manner that you mentally assume that these are intoxicated and drunk for it is the third hour of the day (9:00 a.m.). But this is the thing spoken through the inspired prophet Yow'el (Joel) chapter two verses twenty-eight to thirty-two, *'It will come to pass and exist afterward, I will spill forth My Sacred Breath upon all flesh. Your sons and your daughters will sing and speak by inspiration of predictions. Your old men will dream dreams. Your youth will see revelations. Even upon the male servants and upon the female slaves I will spill forth My Sacred Breath in those days. I will give evidence in the sky where the clouds move and the celestial bodies revolve and upon the earth---blood and fire and cloud columns of smoke. The sun will be changed to darkness and the moon to blood before the coming of the day of the great and revered Yahuah. It will come to pass and exist that all who will call out loud upon the name of Yahuah will be rescued and saved because in Har Tsiyown (Mountain Zion, the Mount of Olives) and in Yruwshalaim (Jerusalem) will be the rescue of salvation just as Yahuah has said and among the survivors whom Yahuah will call.'"*

Kepha (Peter) took a deep breath and continued, "Men of

Yisra'Yah (Israel), hear *HaMachiach* (the Anointed Messiah) Yahusha of Nazareth, a Man from Yahuah having demonstrated among you by miraculous power and miracles and supernatural indications which Yahuah did through Him among you as you also know yourselves. This One by the appointed purpose and forethought of Yahuah given over and surrendered by lawless bands, having impaled on the cross, you murdered, whom Yahuah stood up having loosened the pangs of death because death was not capable to retain Him. For this reason, King David predicted of Yahusha speaking to Yahuah in *Thillah* (Psalm) sixteen verses eight through eleven, **'I eternally put Yahuah before Me for He is My right hand. I will not waver or fall. Therefore, My heart is gleeful and the weight and splendor of My glory rejoices. Also, the flesh of My body will reside permanently in refuge of trust. For You will not relinquish My vitality of breath to Hades, the world of the dead. You will not let Your Holy Messiah to see destruction. You will instruct Me in the road of life and the fullness of glee in front of Your face and the delight at Your right hand of power to the vanishing point of eternity.'** Men, brothers, it is right to say out in public with frankness and bluntness to you with respect to the patriarch David, that both he finished life and expired and was celebrated with funeral rites and his burial place is among us until this day."

Kepha (Peter) continued teaching with power, "Certainly, being an inspired prophet and knowing that with a sworn oath by Yahuah Himself to him that the plucked fruit of his procreative power of the loin with respect on his flesh would stand up the *Machiach* (Anointed Messiah) to sit down on his stately seat on the throne of power. He uttered words with respect to foreseeing the standing up again from the resurrection of death of the *Machiach* (Anointed Messiah) that would not be abandoned in Hades, the place of departed soils or His flesh to see decay. Yahuah stood up this Yahusha of which we all are witnesses. Accordingly, being elevated to the right side of Yahuah and taking a hold of the offering of the announcement of divine assurance of the pledge of the Sacred Breath from the Father, which He has poured forth, this is what you see and hear today."

This statement brought a few murmurs of agreement from the crowd as Kepha (Peter) expanded his words, "For this reason, King David did not go up to the sky but he related in words in *Thillah* (Psalm) one-hundred and ten verse one, **'A poem set to the notes of instrumental music of David. An oracle of Yahuah to My Machiach (Anointed Messiah). Sit at My right hand until I put Your troubling opponents as a footstool to stamp Your feet upon.'** Certainly brothers, let all the family of *Yisra'Yah* (Israel) securely know that Yahuah made Yahusha whom you impaled on the cross both Master and the *HaMachiach* (the Anointed Messiah)."

Having heard this, those in the crowd were pierced thoroughly in the heart of thoughts and feelings and said to Kepha (Peter) and the remaining ambassadors of the Gospel being official commissioners of *HaMachiach* (the Anointed Messiah), "What should we do, men and brothers?" Kepha (Peter) made his thought known and said to them, "Think differently afterwards and reconsider with feelings of compunction and each of you be submerged to make fully wet in baptism upon the authority and character of the name of Yahusha *HaMachiach* (the Anointed Messiah) to the pardon and freedom of sin, and you will take to get a hold of the offering of the gratuity of the Sacred Breath (Holy Spirit). For this reason, the announcement of the divine assurance of the pledge is to you and to your children even to all those at a distant time as many that invites in themselves *HaMachiach* (the Anointed Messiah), our Yahuah."

With many different thoughts and reasoning Kepha (Peter) earnestly attested and implored those in the crowd relating in words,

"Be delivered, saved and protected from this warped and perverse generation of age." Then those who welcomed and took fully what he said were submerged to make fully wet in baptism. There were placed additionally that day about three thousand (3,000) breaths of vitality. They were being earnestly diligent to the instructions of the ambassadors of the Gospel being official commissioners of *HaMachiach* (the Anointed Messiah), in the partnership and in the fracturing of the raised loaves of bread and in the prayers of worship. Every breath came into reverence to their Husband *HaMachiach* (the Anointed Messiah) and many miracles and supernatural indications came into being through the ambassadors of the Gospel being official commissioners of *HaMachiach* (the Anointed Messiah). All those who had faith to entrust their spiritual well-being to *HaMachiach* (the Anointed Messiah) were together and had all things in common and were shared by all. They dispersed as merchandise their acquired estates and their wealth and they distributed to all as much as anyone possessed a requirement for destitution. From day to day they were earnestly diligent with a unanimous mind in breaking raised loaves of bread in the Temple and from dwelling to dwelling they shared and accepted nourishment with a welcome of exultation and simplicity of the heart of thoughts and feelings, praising Yahuah and possessing graciousness of the diving influence upon the heart with all the people. Yahuah placed additionally those being delivered, saved and protected from day to day upon *HaMachiach* (the Anointed Messiah).

That same summer in the year of 30 AD things in Rome were still in an uproar. Caesar Tiberius remained isolated on the Island of Capri and on the throne in Rome sat his advisor and prefect of the Praetorian Guard, Lucius Aelius Sejanus. Sejanus wrote Caesar Tiberius a letter stating, "Dear Exulted Caesar Tiberius, I am compelled to write this letter to you because of a grave matter concerning Agrippina the Elder, the widow of the great general Germanicus who was the grandson-in-law and great nephew of our beloved first Emperor Augustus. It is a matter of recorded history that this union produced nine children: sons-Nero Julius Caesar, Drusus Caesar, Tiberius Julius Caesar who died as an infant, Ignotus who also died as an infant, Gaius the Elder who died in his early childhood, Caligula also known as Gaius the Younger, and daughters-Agrippina the Younger, Julia Drusilla and Julia Livilla. I mention the entire family so that your edict in this soon to be mentioned matter of the State of the Throne can be dealt with in its entirety by your Majesty."

The letter continued, "As you know we have had an undercurrent within the Roman Senate challenging your decision to allow me to handle your day to day affairs on the throne of Rome. This within itself is pure treason against you, the Divine Emperor. After careful investigation by the Imperial Guard it has been discovered that Agrippina the Elder and her two oldest sons, Nero Julius Caesar and Drusus Caesar are the source of unrest amongst the Senators and are secretly plotting against you, our beloved Emperor. Please advise me on how you want me to proceed with this matter since this is a matter against the Throne of the Emperor and not a day to day matter. Your loyal and humble friend and servant, Lucius Aelius Sejanus, Prefect of the Praetorian Gard."

The letter arrived to Caesar Tiberius on the Island of Capri and he had his scribe read the letter to him. By the end of the letter the Emperor was in a fit of rage because he knew that Agrippina the Elder hated Sejanus, even accusing him of assassinating her husband Germanicus while on the battle field. Tiberius jumped up from his stately seat and began pacing back and forth across the floor. What was he to do? What was he to do? He said this over and over in his mind because Agrippina the Elder wielded great power because she was the granddaughter of the first Emperor of Rome, Caesar Augustus. He could not dare to be too obvious with his plot or his kingdom would explode apart. Then he had an idea and commanded his scribe to write the following reply."

"Greetings from your Emperor Caesar Tiberius as witnessed by my royal seal on this scroll. Dear loyal friend Sejanus. Thank you for the recent information and warning about the State of the Throne. As my Prefect of the Praetorian Guard carry out my following orders with swiftness and careful decorum. Give Agrippina an invitation to dine with me as a guest with other stately citizens here on the Island of Capri. Also stage a private meeting of some of the most trusted and powerful Roman Senators and invite her two eldest sons, Nero Julius Caesar and Drusus Caesar to that meeting to discuss the proposal of increasing their interests in the Royal Estate of their great-grandfather Augustus. Their greed will guarantee their attendance to both events. Once Agrippina gets on the boat have the two sons arrested and held in prison until further notice by the Roman Senate. Before Agrippina leaves this Island she shall be imprisoned and all three will be tried by the full Roman Senate for treason and insurrection against the Throne and even the Emperor himself. Since the other four children are so young they pose no threat to my Throne so after two days send the three daughters to me on the Island of Capri and you take young Caligula (Gaius) under your wing of care and instruction. Affixed with my Royal Seal, Emperor Caesar Tiberius."

So early in the fall of 30 AD the royal dinner and the meeting of the Senators were set. Agrippina boarded the boat and the two sons summoned their chariot to attend the legal meeting of the Senators in charge of commerce. Tiberius successfully staged the royal dinner at the imperial palace and Agrippina seemed to be at ease amongst some of her wealthy and prominent society friends. At dinner, Tiberius offered Agrippina an apple as a test of Agrippina's feelings for the Emperor. Agrippina had suspected that the apple could be poisoned and refused to taste the apple. Later that evening she stated to some of the dinner guests that Tiberius tried to poison her. When she tried to board the carriage to take the guests back to the boat dock, it was full and her boarding was refused and was told to wait for the next one just returning up ahead. She looked and could see the light of its lanterns just ahead so she complied. The carriage took off towards the boat dock and the other one arrived within minutes. However, cleverly hidden were royal guards who arrested her and took her to the royal dungeon. Her two sons met the same fate back in Rome at the meeting with the Senators and also were taken to prison to await their trial.

The Roman Senate promptly held a trial later that month and falsely found all three guilty of treason and insurrection against the Throne of the Emperor of Rome. Their sentence was starvation until death. Agrippina the Elder was exiled from the Island of Capri by orders of Caesar Tiberius to the island of Pandataria now called Ventotene in the Tyrrhenian Sea off the coasts of Campania. This island was also the island where her mother was banished and starved to death. On one occasion, under the orders of Tiberius he had a guard flog her severely and during the flogging she lost an eye. Her son Nero Julius Caesar was taken to the Island of Ponza to die of starvation while the other son Drusus Caesar was kept imprisoned in the dungeon at Rome.

How long would it take before Caesar Tiberius found out that the accusations against Agrippina the Elder and her two sons, who were heirs to the throne of Rome were false? Would Caesar Tiberius find out that Sejanus was not his trusted friend but was power hungry and was trying to usurp the throne of Caesar to have the Throne of the Emperor all to himself? Would Sejanus murder the young Caligula (Gaius the younger) since he was the youngest remaining heir to the throne of Rome? How would all this turmoil in the world capital city of Rome affect the Great City of Yruwshalaim (Jerusalem)? These questions are great mysteries that can……..

7

...only be answered by the passage of time. So in the early winter of 31 AD Nero Julius Caesar was forced to commit suicide in the prison on the Island of Ponza. However, the news of his death was never revealed to his mother Agrippina the Elder in the dungeon on the Island of Pandataria now called Ventotene in the Tyrrhenian Sea off the coasts of Campania. Neither was the news given to his brother who was in the dark, damp and stench filled dungeon of Rome itself. In the world outside of prison Sejanus was appointed consul and shared the office with Tiberius *in absentia* (in absence). A consul was the highest elected political office of the Roman Republic and the consulship was considered the highest level of *cursus honorum* (course of offices) which was the sequential order of public offices through which aspiring politicians sought to ascend. Caesar Tiberius had not been in Rome since 26 AD and the senators and wealthy elite counted on the favor of Sejanus as if he were Emperor. Through years of crafty intrigues and indispensable service to the emperor, Sejanus had worked himself up to become the most powerful man in the Roman Empire.

But suddenly, at the end of 31 AD, he was arrested and summarily executed. His downfall began when Antonia the mother of Livilla finally alerted Caesar Tiberius to the growing threat that Sejanus posed in a letter she dispatched to the Island of Capri in the care of her freedman Pallas. When Tiberius heard to what extent Sejanus had already usurped his authority in Rome, he immediately took steps to remove him from power in a letter from the Island of Capri with orders to execute Sejanus without a trial. However, he realized that an outright condemnation could provoke Sejanus to attempt a coup. Instead, Tiberius addressed a number of contradictory letters to the Senate, some of which praised Sejanus and his friends and some of which denounced them. Tiberius variously announced that he would arrive in Rome the next day or that he was at the point of death. He stepped down as consul, forcing Sejanus to do the same and conferred an honorary priesthood upon the young Caligula, rekindling popular support for the house of Germanicus. The ensuing confusion was successful in alienating Sejanus from many of his followers. With the intentions of the emperor no longer clear, it was now deemed a safer course of action at Rome to withdraw from overt support to Sejanus, until the matter was clearly settled.

When it became clear to Tiberius that support for Sejanus was not as strong as the emperor had feared, his next step was to choose Naevius Sutorius Macro the previously prefect of the *vigilus* (Roman police and fire department), to replace Sejanus and effect his downfall. On October 18, 31 AD, Sejanus was summoned to a Senate meeting by a letter from Tiberius, ostensibly to bestow the *tribunician* powers upon him. At dawn, he entered the Senate; but while the letter was being read, Macro assumed control of the Praetorian Guard and members of the *vigiles* led by Graecinius Laco surrounded the building. The senators at first congratulated Sejanus but when the letter, which first digressed into completely unrelated matters, suddenly denounced him and ordered his arrest by Caesar Tiberius, he was immediately surrounded and escorted to prison.

That same evening, the Senate convened at the Temple of Concord and summarily condemned Sejanus to death. He was led from prison and strangled. His body was unceremoniously cast onto the Gemonian Stairs where the crowd tore it to pieces. Riots ensued, in which crowds hunted and killed anyone they could be linked to Sejanus. The Praetorians also resorted to looting when they were accused of having conspired with the former prefect. Following the issue of *damnatio memoriae* (condemnation of memory) by the Senate, his statues were torn down and his name obliterated from all public records. On October 24, Sejanus' eldest son Strabo was arrested and executed. Upon learning of his death, Apicata, the ex-wife of Sejanus and who was divorced so he could marry Livilla, committed suicide on October 26th, after addressing a letter to Tiberius, claiming that Drusus had been poisoned with the complicity of Livilla. The accusations were further corroborated by confessions from Livilla's slaves, who under torture, admitted to having administered the poison to Drusus.

Enraged upon learning the truth about Drusus, Tiberius soon ordered more killings. However, before the killings could begin, Tiberius ordered that Caligula (Gaius the younger) be brought to the Island of Capri safely to the Imperial Palace. Then the remaining children of Sejanus, Capito Aelianus and Junilla, were executed in December of that year. Their bodies were thrown down the Gemonian stairs. At the beginning of the following year, *damnatio memoriae* (condemnation of memory) was passed on Livilla. Although Rome at first rejoiced at the demise of Sejanus, the city quickly plunged into more extensive trials, as Tiberius persecuted all those who could in any way be tied to the schemes of Sejanus or had courted his friendship. The Senatorial ranks were purged; the hardest hit were those families with political ties to the Julians. Even the imperial magistracy was not exempted from Tiberius' wrath. Arrests and executions were now supervised by Naevius Sutorius Macro. The political turmoil would continue for the next six years.

Then in 32 AD on April 28th, Marcus Salvius Otho Caesar

Augustus was born to his father Lucius Otho and his mother Terentia Albia in the town of Ferentinum, Italy (currently Ferento, near Viterbo) in Central Italy. Otho belonged to an ancient and noble Etruscan family, descended from the princes of Ancient Etruri (Central Italy). The following year of 33 AD saw more death in the noble hierarchy of the Roman Empire. In the spring of 33 AD Drusus Caesar died of starvation in a Roman prison even being reduced to eating the stuffing from his bed along with the bugs and rats that dared to cross the interior of his jail cell. Then on October 17th of that same year Agrippina the Elder starved to death on the Island of Pandataria at the young age of 27.

As the calendar rolled on in 34 AD Herod Phillip the Tetrarch of *Iturea* (modern southwest Syria), *Trachonitis* (modern day north east Jordan and northern Saudi Arabia), *Gaulonitis* (also known as Gaul, modern France) and *Paneas* (modern northwest Syria) married his niece Salome, the daughter of his first wife Herodias who divorced him to marry his brother Herod Antipator (Antipas). Salome was the one who danced the dance of the "Seven Vails' at the birthday party of her step-father and then was given the head of Yowchanan Baptista (John the Baptist) on a platter as a reward for pleasing the guests. 34 AD also was the year of the first martyr of those who followed the teaching of Yahusha.

Some of those from the synagogue of assemblage began to debate with Stephanos (Stephen) but they were not able to stand against and oppose the wisdom and the breath with which he talked. Therefore, at that time they introduced unlawfully to give false testimony against him relating in words, "We have heard from him talking impious and scurrilous utterances on matters against Mosheh (Moses) and Yahuah!" These unlawful and false tongued men excited the people and the senior members of the Sanhedrin and the scribes presented themselves and seized Stephanos (Stephen) and brought him in front of the Sanhedrin. They intentionally stood up deceitful and wicked witnesses who testified, "This human being does not quit talking with impious and scurrilous utterances against this sacred location and the Mosaic Law. For this reason, we have heard from him expressing that Yahusha from Nazareth, this One will demolish this place and will make different the habits of law which Mosheh (Moses) entrusted to us!" All those sitting in the Sanhedrin gazed intently at Stephanos (Stephen) and saw his face as though it was the face of an angel.

HaGadowl Kohen (the Chief Priest) asked Stephanos (Stephen), "Do you possess these thoughts and words to be true?" Then he made his thoughts known to them, "I must began with Abraham in Mesopotamia (Iraq) and how Yahuah called him out of that land to possess another. Even when Abraham and his wife Sarah were advanced in years and childless Yahuah said that one day Sarah would conceive and Abraham would have an heir. Yahuah then told Abraham that his seed would be an alien resident in a foreign and hostile land and they would be enslaved to it and would be injured and exasperated for four hundred years. He then gave Abraham the contract of circumcision. In this way Abraham procreated Yitschaq (Isaac) and cut around his sexual organ on the eighth day. Then Yitschaq (Isaac) procreated Ya'aqob (Jacob) who wrestled with Yahuah and Yahuah changed his name to Yisra'Yah (Israel) meaning 'He will rule as Yahuah'. As you know Yisra'Yah procreated the twelve patriarchs and this nation bears his name today."

Stephanos (Stephen) continued his discourse to the *HaGadowl Kohen* (the Chief High Priest) and the members of the Sanhedrin, "Brothers and men of Yisra'Yah (Israel), you know from the sacred scrolls that ten of the patriarchs had very warm feelings against

Yowceph (Joseph) their younger brother and sold him into the hands of *Mitsrayim* (Egypt). Yowceph (Joseph) grew in power and favor with the *Par'oh* (Pharaoh) because of his wisdom and graciousness. *Par'oh* (Pharaoh) eventually designated Yowceph (Joseph) as Supreme Commander with official authority over all *Mitsrayim* (Egypt) second in power only to *Par'oh* (Pharaoh) himself. Then there was an extreme and devastating famine over all the land and only because of the wisdom provided to Yowceph from Yahuah did *Mitsrayim* (Egypt) exist as the only place that had grain for nourishment. Yowceph (Joseph) then brought his entire family from out of the county of *Kna'an* (Canaan) to the country of *Mitsrayim* (Egypt) seventy-five breaths in all."

The members of the Sanhedrin seized and held on to every word of Stephenos (Stephen) as he without flaw or error went through the Torah even with some nodding in agreement with his words, "Then as you, the learned men of the Law know that our people grew in vast numbers in *Mitsrayim* (Egypt) and over centuries of time a new *Par'oh* (Pharaoh) stood up as sovereign who did not know Yowceph (Joseph) or our Yahuah. This one dealt craftily and fraudulently with our kin and injured and exasperated our fathers even to the point of killing all the male infants. At this set and proper time Mosheh (Moses) was born and he was handsome and was hidden and raised in the dwelling of his father for three months. Then his mother put him in a wicker basket and had his sister hide him in the reeds of the Nile River where the daughter of *Par'oh* (Pharoah) found him and adopted him herself as her son. Mosheh (Moses) was educated in all the wisdom of the *Mitsriy* (Egyptians) and was powerful in what was said and in actions. In that manner he was influenced for forty years of time when he thought to inspect his brothers, the sons of Yisra'Yah (Israel)."

You could hear a pin drop in the room as all eyes and ears were totally focused on Stephenos (Stephen) and what he was saying, "As he was inspecting them when he saw one of them being mistreated by one of the *Mitsriy* (Egyptian) task masters wearing the man down with heavy toil and undeserving lashes from the whip. So Mosheh (Moses) rose up and protected the afflicted man and did retribution for him by knocking down the *Mitsriy* (Egyptian) task master fatally with a weapon. Moseh (Moses) deemed that his brothers comprehended that Yahuah through his hand would give to them the deliverance of salvation. But they did not comprehend. Therefore, the very next day, he gazed with wide open eyes two sons of Yisra'Yah (Israel) quarreling and he exhorted them to be in peace saying, 'Men you are brothers, why do you wrong one another?' But the one being unjust to his fellow countryman and shoved him saying, 'Who designated you first in power and rank and a judge over us? Do you not wish to murder me, in the way you murdered the *Mitsriy* (Egyptian) yesterday?' Upon hearing this Mosheh (Moses) ran away and became an alien resident of the land of *Midyan* (Midian) where he procreated two sons."

The power of the Sacred Breath (Holy Spirit) was upon Stephenos (Stephen) as the words of Yahuah seemed to reverberate off the walls, "After a period of forty years, Yahuah appeared to him in the lonesome wasteland of *Har Ciynay* (Mountain Sinai) in a blaze of fire in a brier shrub. Then he heard the voice of Yahuah say to him, 'I Exist as the Yahuah of your fathers, the Yahuah of Abraham and Yitschaq (Isaac) and Yisra'Yah (Israel also known as Jacob). Loosen the sandals under your feet for the spot on which you stand is sacred soil. I have seen and know the maltreatment of My people in *Mitsrayim* (Egypt) and I have heard them sighing and I have descended down to release them. Now come here, I will send you out on a mission to *Mitsrayim* (Egypt).' Thus, Yahuah first in rank and power and a Redeemer sent Mosheh (Moses) out on a mission by the Angel of Yahuah that appeared to him in the Bush. This one, Mosheh (Moses) led our fathers, the people of Yahuah forth doing miracles and supernatural indications in the region of Mitsrayim (Egypt) and in the Red Sea and in the lonesome wasteland for forty years. This is the Mosheh (Moses) who said to the sons of Yisra'Yah (Israel), 'Yahuah will stand up an Inspired Prophet for you from your brothers, like me.'"

At this point in the discourse the voice of Stephenos (Stephen) became stern with great authority, "This is the One who came into being in the congregation in the lonesome wasteland as the Angel speaking to him on *Har Ciynay* (Mountain Sinai) and our fathers who received the living utterances of Yahuah to give to us, to whom our fathers did not prefer to be submissive but rejected and reversed their hearts of feelings and thoughts to *Mitsrayim* (Egypt) as Mosheh (Moses) was getting the tablets of stone from Yahuah on *Har Ciynay* (Mountain Sinai) saying to the brother of Mosheh (Moses), to Aharown (Aaron), 'Make for us gods of gold which will precede and guide us because this Mosheh (Moses) we do not know what has become of him.' Therefore, they made an image of a golden bullock in those days and led up a sacrifice to the heathen god and rejoiced in the works of their hands. They even took up the cloth tent of Moloch the false detestable god of child sacrifice and worshiped the star of the pagan false god *Kiyown* (Rompha) an idol of *Mitsrayim* (Egypt)."

Stephenos (Stephen) continued the narrative, "Yahuah then gave to our fathers the Tent of Tabernacle which became the residence of the Shepherd's Hut to be constructed by the instruction that Yahuah gave to Mosheh (Moses). This is where the glory of Yahuah could dwell between the wings of the Cherubim. When our fathers were on the edge of entering into the Promised Land Mosheh (Moses) sent ten spies out into the land for forty days to bring back a report. Only Kaleb, who was of the ten spies, had the faith to be obedient and enter to possess the Promised Land. However, the other nine stirred our people to unbelief and disobedience to Yahuah and refused to enter as commanded by Mosheh (Moses) and Yahuah. Therefore, our fathers were sentenced by Yahuah to wander and to perish in the lonesome wasteland desert for the next forty years. At the conclusion of forty years Mosheh (Moses) went to be with his fathers and Yhowshua (Joshua) took up the Shepherd's Hut of Tabernacle to receive in occupancy all of the foreign nations whom expelled Yahuah from the face of our fathers until the days of King David."

At the mention of the name of the beloved King David by Stephenos (Stephen) all leaned forward as not to miss a single syllable spilling forth from his lips, "It was at this time when David who had found graciousness in the presence of Yahuah and asked to find an encampment to build a Temple as the residence of Yahuah for the family of Yisra'Yah (Israel). The favor was not granted to King David because of grievous sin but unto his son Shlomoh (Solomon) who constructed a dwelling for Him. But Yahuah does not reside in things of human construction as evidence of the writings of the inspired prophet Yisha'Yah (Isaiah) chapter sixty-six verses one and two, *'Thus says Yahuah, the lofty sky where the celestial bodies revolve is My covered canopied throne and the firm earth the stool of My feet. Where then is the house that you build for Me? Where then is the location of My abode? All these things My hand has made and exist all these things states Yahuah in an oracle.'"*

Then the jaw of Stephenos (Stephen) became tense and he pointed his finger at all those that were hearing his words fall from his lips, "You obstinate and uncircumcised in the heart of feelings and thoughts in the ears, you have always opposed the Sacred Breath (Holy Spirit) as your fathers, also you. Which of the inspired prophets did your fathers not pursue and persecute? They killed outright those who announced beforehand the predicted promise with regard to the coming of *HaMachiach* (the Anointed Messiah) of Whom you now surrendered into the enemy's hands and have become murders, who received the Law by an arrangement of angels, and did not obey it." These words caused an agitation like boiling water among those who were listening to him and a great commotion and loud roar erupted within the chambers of the Temple. When they heard these things their hearts of feelings and thoughts were exasperated and they grated their teeth in rage at him.

But being full of the Sacred Breath (Holy Spirit) he gazed intently into Heaven, the eternal abode of Yahuah, and he saw the glory of Yahuah and Yahusha standing at the right of Yahuah and Stephenos (Stephen) said, "Lo! I am a spectator of the sky having been opened up and the Son of Man standing off the right of Yahuah!" Shrieking and screaming like the croaking of ravens with loud voices and they held over their ears their hands and dashed with one mind upon him. They ejected him from the Temple and drug him outside of the city of Yruwshalaim (Jerusalem) so that they could throw stones at him until he was dead. The witnesses put away their dresses at the feet of a youth under the age of forty years called Sha'uwl (Saul). While they were throwing stones at Stephenos (Stephen) he invoked Yahuah saying, "Yahusha *HaMachiach* (the Anointed Messiah) receive my breath." Then Stephenos (Stephen) placed his knees down to the ground and he exclaimed in a very loud voice, "*Machiach* (Anointed Messiah) do not make stand this sin against them." After speaking these words, he fell asleep and became deceased.

In 36 AD King Aretas IV of the territory of Nabatea (modern day

Jordan, Yemen and Saudi Arabia) where the Bedouin tribes roamed the Arabian Desert declared war on Herod Antipater nicknamed 'Antipas'. This war was to settle boarder disputes in the territories of Perea (Jordan) and Nabatea (Yemen and Saudi Arabia). It was also to settle a personal vendetta of King Aretas IV against Herod Antipater for divorcing his daughter and marrying Herodias, his own sister-in-law. Herod Antipater was soundly defeated so he called upon the aid of Rome by pleading with Caesar Tiberius. Tiberius finally consented and ordered a Roman counter-offensive against King Aretas IV of Nabatea.

Back in Yruwshalaim (Jerusalem) that very year a change in guard also happened in the Temple. The *Parash* (Pharisees) remained in control of the Sanhedrin and the position of *HaGadowl Kohen* (the Chief High Priest). Without much debate or fanfare Jonathan ben Ananus took over the coveted priesthood and would serve in this position until 37 AD. He was of the old regime and cowered to powerful Kaiaphas and his father-in-law Chananyah. He was very corrupt and began to pad his own pockets from out of the Temple Treasury.

One of his main opponents in the election was Sha'uwl (Saul/Paul). He was a thirty-one year old Pharisee whose father was from the tribe of Benjamin and a prominent member of the *Parash* (Pharisee) sect. Sha'uwl (Saul/Paul) had been born in Tarsus, Cilica of the Roman Empire and had been trained from a very young age in the Hillel Rabbinic School by none other than Gamaliel the Elder. Gamaliel in the Hebrew language means 'reward of Yahuah'. He was a Pharisee doctor of Yhuwdiy (Hebrew) Law and the leading authority in the Sanhedrin holding the position as President. Sha'uwl (Saul/Paul) was a member of the group leading the charge to turn Yahusha over to the Romans to be put to death on the cross. His family was close friends of the powerful Kaiaphas and his father-in-law Chananyah but was more of a follower of the religious power than a leader. However, this election defeat made him hungry for political power and the prestige and the monetary gain that went with the position of *HaGawdol Kohen* (the Chief High Priest).

Now at the stoning of Stephenos (Stephen), Sha'uwl (Saul/Paul) guarded at his feet the outside cloaks of those participating in the stoning. He watched intently the throwing of the rocks until Stephenos (Stephen) fell asleep and became deceased. After everyone had picked up their garments, he even threw one last rock upon the lifeless body of Stephenos (Stephen). He even felt gratified with having a part in killing him. It came into being in that day after the death of Stephenos (Stephen) a great persecution on the congregation of the followers of Yahusha in the Great City of Yruwshalaim (Jerusalem). Therefore, the followers of Yahusha distributed themselves in foreign territories, leaving only the ambassadors of the Gospel being official commissioners of *HaMachiach* (the Anointed Messiah) were left in the territory of *Yhuwdah* (Judah) and *Shomrown* (Samaria). Sha'uwl (Saul/Paul) had a brief taste of blood at the stoning and he thirsted for more blood of those who stood against the religious elite and deeply yearned for the excitement of punishing those who practiced or preached a message of good news founded upon Yahusha *HaMachiach* (the Anointed Messiah). To Sha'uwl (Saul/Paul) this was blasphemy against Yahuah and the religious order of the Sanhedrin.

So Sha'uwl (Saul/Paul) requested an appearance with *HaGadowl Kohen* (the Chief High Priest) Jonathan ben Ananus and it was granted to him. Even though Sha'uwl (Saul/Paul) was an apparent challenger to his position as *HaGadowl Kohen* (the Chief High Priest) he did not want to ruffle the feathers of the powerful Gamaliel the Elder or the political machine of Kaiaphas and his father-in-law Chananyah by denying Sha'uwl (Saul/Paul) an audience. After exchanging the usual pleasantries Sha'uul (Saul/Paul) got right to business. He asked Jonathan ben Ananus for written papers with the authority of the Temple to begin to eradicate the followers of Yahusha in the city of Yruwshalaim (Jerusalem). Full permission was granted even including the use of as many Temple Guards as he saw fit to accomplish the eradication. Therefore, Sha'uwl (Saul/Paul) insulted and maltreated the congregation in Yruwshalaim (Jerusalem) by entering dwelling-by-dwelling dragging out both men and women and he surrendered them to the guarded place of the *Kohen* (High Priests).

Since Sha'uwl (Saul/Paul) was so successful in routing out the congregation in Yruwshalaim (Jerusalem) that had become followers of Yahusha, he set his sights on something much bigger. Sha'uwl (Saul/Paul) still was bent upon threats and murder towards the pupils of *HaMachiach* (the Anointed Messiah), and having approached once again to *HaGadowl Kohen* (the Chief High Priest) and asked from him written messages to the city of *Dammeseq* (Damascus, Syria) to the synagogue of the assemblage of persons in the manner that if anyone he found being of the sect called the Road, both men and women, he may bind and bring them to Yruwshalaim (Jerusalem). As he traveled and became near to the city of *Dammesseq* (Damascus, Syria) unexpectedly and suddenly a shining light from Heaven, the eternal abode of Yahuah flashed all around and enveloped him in the light. He fell to the soil and he heard a voice relating in words to him "..................

8

...Sha'uwl (Saul/Paul), Sha'uwl (Saul/Paul)! Why do you pursue to persecute Me?" Sha'uwl kept his face to the ground and covered his face with his hands and whimpering asked, "Who are you sir?" The deep voice like thunder roared, "I EXIST as He, Yahusha, Whom you are pursuing to persecute. Instead, stand up and enter into the town and it will be uttered in words to you, what you must do!" The men traveling in the company of Sha'uwl (Paul) had been standing silent from astonishment, in fact only heard the sound but not even one was a spectator of anything. Then the men went over to Sha'uwl and lifted him up from sitting on the soil but when he opened his eyes he could not look at anyone because he had become blind. They guided him as a blind person by the hand and led him to Dammeseq (Damascus, Syria). He remained there for three days not being able to look at anything and he did not eat or drink.

There was a certain pupil of the Messiah who lived in Dammeseq (Damascus, Syria) by the name of Chananyah (Ananias) and Yahusha HaMachiach (the Anointed Messiah) said to Chananyah (Ananias) in a supernatural spectacle to be gazed at, "Chananyah (Ananias)!" Chananyah (Ananias) answered, "Lo! Here I am Messiah," Then Yahusha said to him, "Stand up and travel on the crowded avenue called Straight and seek in the residence of Yhuwdah (Judas) a man by the name of Sha'uwl (Paul) of the town of Tarseus. For this reason, lo, he is praying to Yahuah and has seen in a supernatural spectacle to be gazed at a man by the name of Chananyah (Ananias) entering and placing on Sha'uwl (Paul) a hand in the manner that he may recover sight."

Chananyah responded, "Messiah, I have heard from many about this man, how many depraved and injurious things he did to Your consecrated ones in Yruwshalaim (Jerusalem). He possesses the privilege of delegated influence here in this spot from the high priests to bind all the ones testifying and worship in Your Name." The Messiah answered him saying, "Travel because this one is a selected vessel to Me to declare the authority and character of My name in the face of foreign nations and sovereigns and sons of Yisra"Yah (Israel). For this reason, I will show him how much it is necessary that he experience the sensation of pain on behalf of My name."

So Chananyah (Ananias) departed and entered into the residence and placed on him his hands saying, "Brother Sha'uwl (Paul) the Messiah Yahusha has sent me out on a mission. He appeared to you on the road which you came in the manner that you may recover sight and be filled with the Sacred Breath." All at once peeling flakes fell of the eyes of Sha'uwl (Paul) and he recovered his sight. Instantly, he stood up and was submerged to make fully wet in baptism. He took the nourishment that was offered to him and was invigorated. Sha'uwl (Paul) was with the pupils in Dammeseq (Damascus, Syria) some days and at once he heralded as a public crier the Divine Truth of the Gospel of the Messiah in the synagogues of the assemblage of persons that this One, Yahusha, is the Son of Yahuah.

All those hearing were put out of wits and became astounded and said, "Is this not the one ravaging and sacking those invoking this name in Yruwshalaim (Jerusalem) and for here in this spot he had come to bind them that he may lead those in front of the high priests?" However, Sha'uwl (Paul) was empowered more and threw the assembly of the Yhuwdiy (Jews) into disorder that lived in the city of Dammeseq (Damascus, Syria) and perplexed their minds that Yahusha is the Messiah. When an ample number of days were satisfied, the Yhuwdiy (Jews) leaders deliberated and determined together to murder him. Their plot became known to Sha'uwl (Paul). The Yhuwdiy (Jews) leaders took note insidiously and scrupulously of the gates both by day and night in the manner that they could murder him. Therefore, the pupils of the Messiah in that city took him away by night and lowered him through the wall, lowering him into the void in a woven lunch hamper receptacle. Sha'uwl (Paul) made very quick haste to Arabia and preached there for three years until 40 AD.

In 37 AD the quiet countryside at the Estates of Arimathea, the daily activities of running the large wealthy estate were interrupted with an air of excitement. Yowceph of Arimathea, the head of the vast estate, was expecting his first child. Yowceph was the great uncle of Yahusha HaMachaiach (the Messiah) and in his younger years was nicknamed Qatan Yow (Little Joe). He had donated the tomb for the Messiah to be laid in and was a leading member of the Sanhedrin. The midwives had been summoned and now all that was left was the anxious waiting for a very nervous father. What seemed to be a lifetime of pacing and nervous small talk with his leading foremen finally came to a sudden halt when one of the midwives stepped forward with a tiny bundle of joy in her arms. An enormous smile cracked the bearded face of Yowceph and tears of great joy and pride welled up in his eyes and began to trickle slowly down his cheeks as he reached for that small package. As soon as he held his first child the midwife announced to those in the room that it was a very healthy little boy. In unrehearsed unison everyone exclaimed, "Halal Yah (Praise to Yahuah)!" On the eighth day, the day of circumcision, Yowceph of Arimathea announced the name of his son was to be

Yowcephas ben Yowceph (Josephus son of Joseph) of Arimathea. Yowcephas (Josephus) would grow up and become one of the greatest and most respected of all historians of Hebrew antiquity. His literary work of *Antiquities of the Jews* was a twenty-volume historiographical work beginning with the creation of Adam and Eve and ending with the Jewish War.

However back in Rome, the mood was a mixture of sadness and elation that same year of 37 AD. Caesar Tiberius died on March 16th at the age of seventy-seven years old. Immediately Caligula, the great nephew of Emperor Tiberius was named as the new Caesar. His proper name was Gaius Julius Caesar Augustus Germanicus from the house of the Julio-Claudian dynasty. Early in his reign he was noble and a moderate ruler. However after the first six months of his reign he became known for his cruelty, sadism, extravagance and sexual perversity. He became known as the insane tyrant. That same year on December 15th, in Antium (Modern day Anzio-Nettuno Italy) a son was born to Gnaeus Domitius Ahenobarbus Cladius and Agrippina the Younger, the great granddaughter of Caesar Augustus and sister of Emperor Caligula and they named him Nero Claudius Caesar Augustus Germanicus.

The great city of Yruwshalaim (Jerusalem) was also not without excitement in 37 AD with the good news of the death of Caesar Tiberius. The Temple elected a new *HaGadowl Kohen* (the High Priest) in the Sanhedrin. A *Parash* (Pharisee) was selected to replace Jonathan ben Ananus. The successor named was Theophilus ben Ananus (Theophilus son of Ananus) who was a member of the wealthiest and most influential Hebrew families in all of Yhuwdah (Judean Province). He was the brother of the previous *Gadowl Kohen* (High Priest) and the brother-in-law of Yowceph Caiaphias, the High Priest that Yahusha the Messiah appeared in front of to be condemned by the few hand-selected members of the Sanhedrin before being turned over to Pilate.

Two years later in 39 AD, it seemed to be a normal day in the Great City of Yruwshalam (Jerusalem) when all of a sudden a fast galloping horse with a public crier came through the center northern gates screaming, "News from Rome! News from Rome! *Shama Yhuwdi* (hear oh Jews), *Shama Yhuwdi* (hear oh Jews), news from Rome!" As the rider approached the town square a very large crowd began to gather. Roman soldiers on patrol became wary of the ever growing crowd and sent word for back up patrols in case of trouble. After the crowd was somewhat silenced so that they could hear the public crier, he began to address the crowd.

He began to read from his scroll, "To those in the territory ruled by Rome under the supreme guidance of the throne of Caesar Caligula. Today I announce that Herod Antipater also known as Herold Antipas has died." A cheer and whistling interrupted the public crier's speech for a moment but then quieted down so they could hear more of the news. The crier continued, "The throne of Rome would like to elaborate that shortly after Caesar Caligula bestowed the title of "king" to Herod Antipas, the brother of his wife Herodias, Agrippa, presented to Caesar Caligula a list of charges against the tetrarch including that he conspired against the late Caesar Tiberius with Sejanus and was currently plotting against Caesar Caligula with Artabanus. Evidence was presented that Herod Antipas had amassed a massive stockpile of weaponry sufficient to equip seventy-thousand (70,000) soldiers. Therefore all of the money and territory of Herod Antipas was turned over to Agrippa and Herod Antipas was exiled to Lugdunum Gaul (modern Lyon, France). Herodias was allowed to keep her property by Caesar but instead she refused and chose to join her husband Herod Antipas in exile where he died." The large crowd became unruly in their celebration so they were quickly dispersed by Roman Calvary and foot soldiers with riot gear. Twelve year old Yiramiah Aer (Jerry Ayers) had been to the lower market and quickly went home to the Upper City to report the news of the public crier to his parents and neighbors.

Also, in Rome that year of 39 AD the father of two-year old Nero died and his mother was exiled. Then very young Nero was sent to his aunt to raise him. In addition, a very important birth took place in Rome. Born that year was Titus Flavius Caesar Vespasianus Augustus. He was a member of the Flavian Dynasty. Thirty-one years later as Emperor he would besiege Yruwshalam (Jerusalem) and destroy the Second Temple in 70 AD.

In 40 AD Sha'uwl (Paul) decided to leave Arabia and journey back to the Great City of Yruwshalaim (Jerusalem). Sha'uwl (Paul) after a long trip finally arrived in Yruwshalaim (Jerusalem) and he attempted to be glued to the pupils there but all were frightened of him because they did not have faith that he entrusted his spiritual well-being to the Messiah and that he was now a pupil of the Messiah Yahusha. But one man named Bar-abiy (Barnabas) seized him and led him to the ambassadors of the Gospel being official commissioners of the Messiah and related fully to them in what way he saw the Messiah on the road and that the Messiah Yahusha had talked to him. Also, in what way in Dammeseq (Damascus, Syria) he was frank in utterance and confident full of the Sacred Breath in the authority and character of Yahusha.

Sha'uwl (Paul) talked and discussed by investigating jointly with the Hellenistes (Greek speaking Jews) but they tried to put their hands on him to murder him. The brothers became acquainted with this situation and led him down to the city of Kaisereia (Caesarea) and dismissed him to the city of Tarsos (Tarsus) where he would be safe to begin his ministry.

That very year while Sha'uwl (Paul) was getting established in his ministry in the city of Tarsos (Tarsus) the Roman Empire began to expand again. Caesar Caligula learned of the news that the Ptolemy of the country of ancient Mauretania had died. The territory of Mauretania in Northern Africa (modern Morocco) had been a client state of the Roman Empire since 33 B.C. by orders of Julius Caesar. Now that the Ptolemy was dead Caesar Caligula seized the moment and sent a large delegation to the mourning country and made them part of the Roman Province. The people of Mauretania were no longer an independent client state but were now subject to the full rule of the throne in Rome.

The palace in Rome was also full of excitement that year in 40 A.D. as Claudius, the uncle of Caesar Caligula announced that the royal family added another member. Claudius was the proud father of baby daughter Claudia Octavia who one day would become the first wife of Caesar Nero. She was the great niece of the deceased Emperor Tiberius and the paternal first cousin of the current Caesar Caligula. A large celebration was held at the palace in Rome by Caesar Caligula in honor of his uncle Claudius.

Rome was not the only place that held a celebration that year, but an important celebration was held back in the Great City of Yruwshalaim (Jerusalem). It was the eve of the *bar mitzvah* for Yiramiah Aer (Jerry Ayers). Yes, Yiramiah Achuw Aer (Jerry Lee Ayers) would turn thirteen years old this year to reach a major milestone in his young life. *Bar Mitzvah* translates to "son of commandment", *bar* means "son" and *mitzvah* means "commandment". At the age of thirteen all Hebrew boys become a *bar mitzvah* (son of commandment) thus becoming fully accountable to the *Torah Law* as an adult. He had been working very hard for the past eighteen months under the guidance of Yowchanan (John) preparing for this important day.

As Ya'kov Aer (James Ayers) the fan maker sat down at the supper table that evening, he said in a firm questioning voice, "Wife, do you know what tomorrow is?" At the sound of this question, twelve year old Yiramiah Aer sat up with a huge grin on his face and with wide open eyes peered at his mother in anticipation of her answer. "Why yes, let's see here. Today is the twenty-third day of *Tammuz* (July 17), so tomorrow would be the twenty-fourth day of *Tammuz* (July 18)" she answered. Yiramiah let out a little giggle which brought a quick look in his direction from his father. Then Ya'kov Aer (James Ayers) continued with his questions, "So wife, do you have anything special planned for tomorrow?" Once again, Yiramiah looked at his mother in anticipation of her response. She answered, "Let's see, I have laundry to do in the morning before the lunch baking, I need to dust and clean the front part of the house and oh, us neighborhood women are planning to go to the market in the afternoon. Why do you ask? Do you need something special from the market?" "No, nothing special, I guess."

This conversation was so exasperating for young Yiramiah that he could hardly contain himself. He continued to sit in silence as a means of respect for the adults at the table while they were having a conversation. However, at the last response of his father, he was beyond containment and he threw both of his hands over his face. Then Ya'kov Aer (James Ayers) turned his head towards his son and asked, "Are you feeling well, my son? You haven't touched any of the food on your plate and now you grasp your face with both hands." Yiramiah quickly answered, "I feel fine *ab* (father). I know what tomorrow is. It's …" Yakov interrupted his son and said, "*Ken, ken* (Yes, yes) I know it is the twenty-fourth day of *Tammuz* (July).

Your mother has already told me." Yiramiah was just beside himself and began to make his case, "*Ab* (father) but, but.." Then his mother interrupted Yiramiah, "Now Yiramiah we have already gone over the calendar so please eat your supper and we can discuss this when your plate is all clean."

Ya'kov looked at his wife and they both smiled as Yiramiah began to hastily consume the food on his plate. Ya'kov could hardly stand to remain silent without teasing his son, so he blurted out, "You know wife, I have it in the back of my mind that tomorrow I have something special planned. Do you remember anything special happening tomorrow?" Yiramiah quickly jerked up his head and looked at his mother across the table. She replied, "Well, let me think. Other than planning on going to the market, I don't have anything. Do you have any fan orders that need to be completed and delivered?" Ya'kov answered, "Yes, I am working on a couple of large fans for Pilot but they are not due until next month." Ya'kov then looked at his son who was about to explode and asked, "*Ben* (son) do you having anything special planned for tomorrow?"

Yiramiah threw both arms in the air and with frustration blurted out, "Tomorrow I am *bar mitzvah* (son of commandment)! It is my thirteenth birthday!" Ya'kov Aer (James Ayers) said to his wife, "What do you know about this?" His wife looked at Yiramiah and questioned, "Are you sure son? How could this happen so soon?" Yiramiah was beyond belief that his parents would forget such an important day in his life and said, "Mother, it has been thirteen years getting here and you both know how hard I have been working with Yowchanan these past eighteen months getting ready for this day." Then Ya'kov got up and stood above the reclining Yiramiah and with both hands grasped both sides of his head. Then he kissed the top of the head of Yiramiah and said with teary eyes, "My son we did not forget. We are both so proud of you. Your mother and I have a very special day planned tomorrow for you that you will never forget. As our little ambitious boy begins to become a man of Yahuah it is hard to turn loose of our baby and turn him over totally to Yahuah for manhood. Our wish is that you will always remember tomorrow and someday pass on a very special day to your son when he becomes *bar mitzvah* (son of commandment)." Yiramiah jumped up from his reclining position and embraced his father with both arms in a tight embrace. His mother who was reclining across the table began to weep with a bursting heart of joy and a sense of pride as tall as the tallest mountain.

Then the soon-to-be teenage Yiramiah pulled his head away from his father's chest and looked into his father's moist eyes as warm salty tears were flowing down both their cheeks. Yiramiah (Jerry) spoke in a soft and quivering voice, "*Ab* (father) I love you and mother so much and in my heart I will always be your little curly haired ambitious boy. Maybe your feelings are like when Yahuah gave His only Son, Yahusha to mankind. It was probably hard for Yahuah to see Yahusha grow up because He knew that His Son would die on that horrible cross. But don't worry father, Yahuah will take good care of me when I become totally His tomorrow and become *bar mitzvah* (son of commandment)."

Ya'kov (James) clinched his son Yiramiah back to his chest and said, "Son your spiritual wisdom and insight never ceases to amaze me. Your mother and I are so proud to be your parents. I know that tomorrow the angels in heaven will sing songs of great and joyous praise because Yahuah has gained a mighty warrior and defender of His Torah in celebration of you becoming a *bar mitzvah* (son of commandment)." By now the mother of Yiramiah (Jerry) had joined them and the family stood there frozen in time embracing in a group hug of the purest family love shared between a child and his parents.

The flames on the candles began to flicker and the light in the room began to grow dim yet no one wanted to be the first to release their hold on that precious moment in time. Finally, after a few sniffles, Ya'kov (James) spoke up and said, "You know, there is a very special young man in this room who has a very big day ahead of him tomorrow. I think it is time for him to go to bed and get some good rest so that he will be able to endure all the celebration and activities of becoming *bar mitzvah* (son of commandment). Now off to bed with you!" So...

9

...Yiramiah (Jerry) kissed his father and mother good night and headed to his room and laid down on his straw mattress. He gazed intently out the lattice window into the pitch black sky decorated with thousands of gleaming stars. He was emotionally exhausted but his inquisitive mind would not shut off. Therefore, he just laid there pondering and cherishing the events of the evening which stirred the emotions of excitement for all the activities of celebration which would unfold during the entire day tomorrow in his honor. What seemed like hours was actually only minutes before the bright dancing stars rocked his heavy eyelids closed and sent Yiramiah into the peaceful sleep of dream land.

The next thing Yiramiah knew was that his bed was surrounded by Roman soldiers screaming, "You are under arrest!" Two soldiers were on each side of the bed banging their huge round golden shields with their long wooden spears. At the foot of the bed stood the Roman Captain with red plumage extending down the center from the front to the back of his helmet. He had a hold of his legs trying to drag him out of bed as he was yelling, "You are under arrest! The charges against you are sedation against the throne of Caesar in Rome and inciting a riot amongst the Hebrew priesthood in the city of Yruwshalaim (Jerusalem) claiming to be *bar mitzvah* (son of commandment) and a follower of the dead Yahusha. Now get up or I will drag you all the way to the garrison for your execution!" Then the beating on the shields with the long pointed spears kept getting louder and faster as the Roman soldiers mocked him in laughter shouting in mockery, "*Mazal tov bar mitzvah* (Good luck son of commandment)." They repeated this over and over and faster and faster and louder and louder and finally the Roman Captain pulled him off his straw mattress as he hit the wooden floor with a thud. He closed his eyes as the Roman Captain pulled out his gleaming silver sword from its sheath and raised it to strike Yiramiah.

However, he did not feel the double-edged sword strike him anywhere so he slowly cracked open his eyes. To his surprise standing over him was not the Roman Captain but it was his mother laughing hysterically and his father beating a copper pan with a long handled wooden spoon shouting at the top of his lungs, "Enough rest, *mazal tov bar mitzvah* (good luck son of commandment)." He was so happy to see them instead of the Roman soldiers who apparently were in his dream that he jumped up from the floor and gave each one of them a big hug. Then he shared his dream of how the Roman soldiers were beating their spears against their shields saying *mazal tov bar mitzvah* and the Roman Captain yelling, "You are under arrest!" When all along it was his dad beating that copper pan with the wooden spoon yelling, "Enough rest *mazal tov bar mitzvah!*" All three of them got a big laughter out of the event and then they ate breakfast and got ready to go to the synagogue for the ceremony.

Since they lived in the Upper City of *Yruwshalaim* (Jerusalem) they had many friends and neighbors and Ya'kov was a well-known and respected businessman both to the Romans and the Hebrews alike. Therefore, as they traveled to the synagogue many who saw them shouted *mazel tov* (good luck). First, they passed the house of Caiaphas and took the eastern streets to avoid going by the old Palace of Herod and the Hasmonoean Palace. The synagogue that they were going to was just west of the Temple and south of the Xystus Market and the bridge leading to the Royal Porch of the Temple. When they arrived, standing there to greet them was Yowchanan (John) and his brother Ya'kov (James) the two cousins of Yahusha the Messiah.

Before they entered into the synagogue Ya'kov the disciple of Yahusha asked to pray for this small family. Ya'kov Aer (James Ayers) agreed and had Yiramiah stand in front of him putting his hand upon the shoulders of Yiramiah. The mother of Yiramiah stood by her husband and Ya'kov the disciple stood in front of them with his right hand on the shoulder of Ya'kov Aer and his left hand on the shoulder of his wife. Then he began to pray, "Oh, Yahuah Creator of life and giver of blessings to those who believe in the name of your Son Yahusha. Today, I ask a special blessing from you to come upon this devoted family. Their little boy has now began the life-long journey of *bar mitzvah* (son of commandment) the first step into adulthood. Continue to guide his parents with his upbringing and spreading the news of how your Son Yahusha was crucified and rose again on the third day proving that He was *HaMachiach* (the Anointed), the Messiah spoken of in the Torah Law and the *haftarah*. May You give Yiramiah peace in his heart and mind as he fulfills the ceremony of *bar mitzvah* today. I ask these things in the name of Yahusha HaMachiach. *Halal Yah* (Praise to Yahuah)."

After the prayer, they all went inside the synagogue and greeted the guests who had already arrived. Then they took their assigned seats and waited for the ceremony to begin. When it was time for the ceremony to begin, Yowchanan (John) the favorite disciple of Yahusha and the chosen instructor for Yiramiah signaled that it was time for everyone to put on their *tallit* (prayer shawl). The *tallit* (prayer shawl) was a woolen rectangular cloth decorated with black lines across each bottom quarter of the *tallit* with black strings called *tzitzit* tied in a series of knots on each of the four corners. The purpose of the *tzitzit* serve as a reminder of the duties and obligations of a Hebrew.

The congregation put their *tallis* (prayer shawls) on the top of their heads and all began to sing acapella the song of the *tallit*. "*Baruch atah Yahuah, Eloheinu melech ha olam, Asher kidishanu b'mitzvotav, Vitzivanu l'hitatef b'tzitzit.* (Blessed are you Lord our Yahuah, Ruler of the Universe, Who has sanctified us with your mitzvoth and commanded us to wrap ourselves in tzitzit)." Then Yowchanan (John) continued with the ceremony with an opening prayer, "Yahuah, Giver of eternal life we come to You and ask a special blessing upon this joyous celebration. Allow the Sacred Breath to hover and move our hearts closer to You as we join in the celebration with Yiramiah Aer (Jerry Ayers) and his family on this momentous occasion. *Halal Yah* (Praise to Yahuah)." Then all in the congregation responded, "*Halal Yah* (Praise to Yahuah)."

Following the prayer, Yowchanan (John) announced, "It is now time for the *aliyah* (ascent) of Ya'kov Aer (James Ayers) and his wife." The *aliyah* (ascent) not only represented the physical ascent onto the platform in front of the congregation but also referred to the spiritual elevation experienced at that time. The practice of *aliyah* (ascent) or 'going up' was symbolic of the nation of Yisra'Yah (Israel) 'going up' from the land of *Mitsrayim* (Egypt) to the Promise Land. The wife of Ya'kov Aer carried a bundle neatly wrapped in a white sheet. When they stepped onto the platform she unfolded it and stood next to her husband Ya'kov (James). Then Yowchanan (John) said to the congregation, "Now, I call upon *bar mitzvah* (son of commandment) Yiramiah Aer (Jerry Ayers) to take his first *aliyah* (ascent) and join us on the platform."

Yiramiah (Jerry) smiled at Yowchanan (John) and made his first *aliyah* to the platform in front of the congregation. He then took his place and stood between his father and Yowchanan (John). Next, Ya'kov (James) his father reached to the bundle that his wife was holding and retrieved a neatly folded *tallit* (prayer shawl). He unfolded the *tallit* (prayer shawl) and placed it behind the neck of Yiramiah draping it over the front of his shoulders and the inside of his forearms. Then Ya'kov (James) said to his son, "Yiramiah I present to you your *tallit* (prayer shawl) as commanded in the book of *Bamidbar* meaning 'the desert' (Numbers) chapter fifteen verses thirty-seven and thirty-eight, " **Yahuah spoke this arrangement of words to Mosheh (Moses) saying, speak this arrangement of words to the sons of Yisra'Yah (Israel) and must say to them that they must make for themselves tassels of wing-like projections on the extreme edges of their tallit (prayer shawls) for their generation of revolution of time. They must put on the tzitzit (tassel) of wing-like projections of the extreme edge a twine of violet-blue, the color of the cerulean mussel."** Then his father and mother kissed him on both cheeks.

Next, Yowchanan (John) stepped in front of the mother of Yiramiah and also retrieved an item from the bundle she was holding. He then returned back to his spot standing next to Yiramiah and placed the *tefillin* on the head and arms of Yiramiah. *Tefillin* are black leather boxes containing parchments inscribed with the *Shema* (the hearing) and other biblical passages. Yowchanan (John) said to Yiramiah, "Yiramiah I have placed upon you your *tefillin* (leather boxes of scripture) on your head and arms as required by the Torah Law in the book of *Dabar* meaning 'the spoken words' (Deuteronomy) chapter six verse eight, **"You must physically tie them on the open hand of power as a signal and evidence. They shall exist for a filler for the forehead between your eyes."** Now *bar mitzvah* (son of commandment) Yiramiah tell the congregation what verses you have chosen for your *tefillin* (leather boxes of scripture) and recite them out loud."

Yiramiah grinning from ear to ear announced, "I have actually chosen three that are dear to my heart. The first is *Ha Shema* (the hearing) found in the book of *Dabar* meaning 'the spoken words' chapter six verse four, **"Shema Yisra'Yah Yahuah Yah Yahuah Echad (Hear oh Israel, Yahuah is our God, Yahuah is One."** The second is *Ha Gadowl Mitsvah* (The Greatest Command) also found in the book of *Dabar* meaning 'the spoken words' chapter six verse five, **"Ahab Yahuah Yah, kol lebab, kol nephesh, kol m'od. (Love Yahuah your God with all your heart and with all your vitality of breath and with your whole strength."** My third and final verse that I have chosen to include in my *tefillin* is found in the book of *Yhowshua* meaning 'Yahuah saved' (Joshua) chapter twenty-four verse fifteen, **"But as for me and my house we shall serve Yahuah!"** I pledge to Yahuah and to this congregation that these three verses shall be the cornerstone of my life."

Yowchanan (John) dismissed the mother of Yiramiah from the platform and she returned to her seat. Then, Yowchanan handed the Torah Scroll to Ya'kov Aer (James Ayers). Ya'kov Aer (James Ayers) handed the Torah Scroll to Yiramiah and said, "It is with great honor and pride as your father to hand you this Torah Scroll on your first *aliyah* (ascent). At my first *aliyah* (ascent) your great-grandfather Ya'kov Melek Beyth Aer (James Henry Ayers) handed it to your grandfather Chizqiy Aer (Charles Ayers) who then handed it to me. If they were alive today they too would join in the generational handing down of the Torah Law to you. Now I have handed the Torah Law to you as a *bar mitzvah* (son of commandment) and Yowchanan has passed you to be the *Olim* (the one who makes the ascent) the reader of the law on this *aliyah* (ascent). You shall now stand alone with Yahuah." At the end of this speech both Ya'kov (James) and Yowchanan joined the congregation and sat down.

Then Yiramiah (Jerry) opened up the Torah Scroll and said, "My Torah reading is a song of Mosheh (Moses) found in the book of *Dabar* meaning 'the spoken words' (Deuteronomy) chapter thirty-two verses one through fifteen, **"Broaden out your ears and listen oh lofty sky where the clouds move and the celestial bodies revolve and I will speak an arrangement of words. Listen intelligently and pay attention, oh firm earth to something said from the speech of my mouth. My instruction will drip like rain. The things said in my speech will trickle like the dew of a shower upon the sprouting grass and like the accumulation of the drops of rain on the glistening green grass because I will call out the honor, authority and character of Yahuah. Give magnitude to our Yah! He is the Rock of refuge. His work is truth full of integrity because His trodden roads as a course of life are a pronounced judicial verdict of divine decrees. A Yah of firm moral fidelity and security and there does not exist evil. He is just and straight. He has not brought ruin and decay to Himself but to His sons it is their blemish. A distorted, false and crafty tortuous generation of revolution of time!"**

"Do you treat with ill Yahuah like this? Oh stupid, impious and wicked people, you are not wise. Is He not your Father who created and purchased you? Has He not made you and established you? Remember the days of sunset to sunset of the past, mentally understand the years of revolution of time of past generations. Inquire and request of Your Father and He will explain it by word of mouth like an announcement. You're old, they will tell you. When Yahuah divided their inheritance to the foreign nations for distribution, when He separated and spread the sons of red fleshed human beings, He stationed the boundaries and regions of the peoples according to the number of the sons of Yisra'Yah

because Yahuah's allotment is His people. Yisra'Yah is the district of his inheritance. He found him in a desert land and in the desolated wasteland, a howling desolation. He surrounded him and separated him for understanding. He protected him like the little man of His eye. Just like the eagle who wakes up its nest and broods over its nestlings being nude of feathers. It breaks apart its flapping wings, takes it and lifts it on its wing. Yahuah alone guided him and there did not exist with him a foreign el (pagan god). He made him ride on the elevated places of the firm earth and he ate the produce of the spread out flat fields. He made him suck the sticky gummy syrup of honey from the craggy rock and the rich perfumed olive oil from the hard flint rocky cliff."

"Curdled milk and cheese of beef cattle and the rich milk of the migrating flocks of sheep and goats, with the richest and choicest fat of plump rams and strong rams of the sons of Bashan. Also full grown the goats with the richest fat of the kidneys of wheat and you did drink of the blood of the grape as fermented wine! But Yisra'Yah (Israel) grew oily and gross with fat and despised Me. He grew oily and gross with fat, dense and covered with flesh. He rejected Yah who made him and despised with wicked disgrace the Rock of His Yahusha."

The congregation was silent during the reading until the last sentence and then there were a few moans and groans. Yiramiah (Jerry) rerolled the scroll and handed it back to Yowchanan (John) as Yowchanan approached the front of the congregation but did not go up on the platform and he said, "Now Yiramiah will chant the *haftarah* (taking leave) from the *Nev'im* (prophets) following that inspirational reading of the Torah Law."

Yiramiah looked over the congregation and said, "For the *haftarah* (taking leave) I have chosen a section from the book of the great prophet Ysha'Yah meaning 'Yahuah has Saved' (Isaiah) chapter fifty-three verses one through ten" Even though the voice of Yiramiah was changing he still had a beautiful teenage soprano voice that could spell bind any audience. He looked at this father Ya'kov (James) with a big smile and began the melodious chant of sweet musical notes as he sang the *haftarah* (taking leave).

"Who has believed our announcement? To whom is the arm of Yahuah revealed? Because He comes up as a tender shoot in front of His face and as a root from out of the dry red soil. The form of an outline or figure does not belong to Him, and His majesty is not that we should see Him and a handsome appearance that we should delight in. Disesteemed, destitute and rejected by men, a son of anguish from affliction and known of malady and anxiety. Also, as keeping secret of faces from Him. Being disesteemed and we did not value or regard Him. Surely our maladies, anxieties and calamities He has born and our anguish from affliction He carried them. But we did not regard or value Him, violently struck and punished being stricken severely by Yahuah and afflicted. But He was wounded by boring through Him for our religious and moral revolt, cracked to pieces for our perverse evil. The chastisement as a warning and instruction of our peace was on Him .With His stripes and welts and black and blue marks we ourselves are mended and cured."

"We all are like sheep having gone astray. Each man to his trodden road as a course of life we have turned. Yahuah has made to impinge violence on Him for the perverse evil of us all. He was harassed and oppressed and He was browbeaten but He did not open His mouth. As a member of the flock He was brought to the slaughter. Also, as a ewe in the front of her shearers His tongue tied so He does not open His mouth. From the constraint of prison and from justice He was taken and His generation of revolution of age who will ponder? Because He was cut off from the land of the living. From the moral and

religious revolt of My people, the blow of infliction was on Him. He was put with the morally wrong His grave sepulcher and with a rich man in His death. Though He had not done any violence or wrong and deceiving fraud was not in His mouth. But Yahuah desired as a valuable thing to bruise Him and to make Him weak, afflicted and grieved. If He will put the punishment of guilt on His vitality of breath He will see seed to be planted and He will make long days of sunset to sunset and the desire of Yahuah in His hand will prosper and push forward." Amen (So be it) Amen (So be it)!"

Some of the Hebrew scholars in the congregation gasped when Yiramiah (Jerry) used a double *Amen* (So be it) to close the *haftarah* (taking leave). You see the *Talmud* (written opinions of Rabbinical Law) teaches that the Hebrew word *Amen* comes from an acronym of a Hebrew phrase *El Melek Ne'aman* (Almighty Yahuah, King is Faithful). Also, by repeating it twice, the *Amen* (So be it) became a witness to truth and since the witness came at the end of a phrase it had eternal implications.

Then Ya'kov (James) the disciple and leader of the followers of Yahusha *HaMachiach* (the Anointed or the Messiah) took his *aliyah* (ascend) and stood on the platform to dismiss the congregation with a benediction. He chose to recite from the book of *BaMidbar* meaning 'in the desert wilderness' (Numbers) chapter six verses twenty-four to twenty-seven, **"Yahuah barak shamar. Yahuah owr paniym el chanan. Yahuah nasa paniym suwm shalowm. Suwm shem, Yahuah, al bens Yisra'Yah. Aniy, Aniy barak. (May Yahuah bless you and put a hedge of thorns about to guard and protect you. May Yahuah cause to illuminate His face upon you and stoop and bend in kindness and favor to you even though you are inferior. May Yahuah lift up His face to you and give you shalom of safety, happiness, health, prosperity** *and peace. So they will put My name, Yahuah on the sons of Israel. And I, I will bless them.)"*

After the benediction, the congregation was invited to go to the house of Ya'kov Aer (James Ayers) for the reception and to continue the celebration of Yiramiah (Jerry) becoming *bar mitzvah* (son of commandment).

10

While the ceremony was taking place in the synagogue, many of the neighboring women decorated the house and courtyard of the fan maker Ya'kov Aer (James Ayers). They set up and prepared several long tables of delicious food that was customary for this type of celebration. They were just putting on the finishing touches as Ya'kov Aer (James Ayers), his wife, Yiramiah (Jerry) and the first of the invited guests began to show up. Yiramiah (Jerry) stopped at the gate of the courtyard and marveled at all the decorations to set a festive tone for this joyous occasion.

There were several wooden poles standing six foot high with two foot strips of cloth attached at the top in a multi-hue of colors. Red, blue, yellow, orange and green pieces of cloth waved in the slight gentle breeze blowing from the south. Large canopies of blue cloth fluttered in the gentle breeze that were draped overhead the vast tables of food matching the clear blue cloudless sky above. In the corner of the courtyard with the backdrop of several large violet and dark blue with pink centered 'Rose of Sharon' bushes also called 'Hibiscus' was a harpist strumming and plucking gentle and soothing music from the strings on her harp. The soft melodious notes seemed to just float in the gentle breeze wrapping all the guests in a sense of peace and tranquility.

As Yiramiah (Jerry) walked by the vast tables of food the first thing he saw was several large bowls of *hummus*. This was a favorite creamy dip made up of chickpeas, tahini-a paste made from sesame seeds, olive oil, lemon juice and garlic. Next to the hummus were several types of freshly baked crispy breads thinly-sliced and ready for dipping into the hummus. Then there were a large variety of baked and boiled *bagels* filled with lox which is salmon filets that have been cured and cold smoked. Other variety of bagels were filled with whitefish, dill, red onion and pickled capers that taste like salty green olives. Next on the table were four large platters of *rugelach*, a mouthwatering treat of a flaky pastry spread with cinnamon sugar and chocolate chips or a variety of jams that had been rolled and baked.

The mouth of Yiramiah (Jerry) began to water and his stomach began to growl as he continued the tour of the long line of delicious cuisine. The next item on the table was several types of *knish*-a kind of turnover baked or deep fried. Some were filled with mashed potatoes and others were filled with ground meat, sauerkraut, onions, cheese and even some filled with *kasha* (buckwheat groats). Then there were three twelve inch circular loaves of chopped liver. These loaves were a mixture of finely chopped goose and chicken livers seasoned with *schmaltz* (rendered chicken fat), coarsely chopped onion, diced hardboiled eggs, salt, cracked black pepper, and *gribenes* (the crispy cracklings created during the *schmaltz* collecting process). Then the liver loaf is garnished with fresh bright green minced parsley. This delicious meat dish was followed with pans of cooked *farfel*-small pellet-shaped egg noodle pasta.

One of the most favorite dishes came next which was loaves of homemade *challah* bread. These oval shaped freshly baked braided loaves of egg bread with their dark brown braided round tops and their yellowish-tan side braids had their own tantalizing aroma that made any stomach grumble with intense hunger. However, the aromatic aroma emitting for the next platters sent the taste buds of Yiramiah (Jerry) into an uncontrolled lustful tizzy. There were platters of heaping mountains of braised brisket just lying there begging to be eaten. The brisket was first browned in a skillet over a fire in fresh olive oil. Then it was placed in a pot over the fire smothered with aromatic spices and vegetables. Yiramiah (Jerry) could see the onions, finely chopped garlic, fresh dark green bay leaves, diced celery, thinly sliced carrots and diced tomatoes. The entire pot was allowed to simmer and bathe until tender and done in a rich red wine. When it was placed on the platter ready for serving it was garnished with bright green parsley leaves. Yiramiah (Jerry) could not help himself and he tore off a small piece of brisket and quickly put it in his mouth which drew a glare from one of the women passing by with a bowl of the last item to go on the table. It was a large pot of *matzah* ball soup. This was a pot of chicken soup which bathed many dumplings made out of matzah meal, eggs and *schmaltz* (rendered chicken fat). What a feast Yiramiah (Jerry) thought to himself as the tantalizing aroma of the food enticed his taste buds driving his hunger pangs into an uncontrollable rumblings like the sound of mighty thunder echoing across the eastern wall of Yruwshalaim (Jerusalem) on the Mount of Olives.

His wandering thoughts were interrupted by the anxious sound of the voice of his father Ya'kov (James) sending his senses of sight and sound quickly searching for the location of that familiar tone. His mind quickly focused on the calling of, "Yiramiah. Yiramiah my son. Come here and join me," was the beckoning call of his father. Yiramiah quickly ran to where his father was standing and Ya'kov motioned for quiet with his arms while requesting, "*Shaqat! Shaqat! Be'vakasha shaqat!* (Be quiet! Be quiet! Please be quiet!" When the crowd of guests became quiet and focused their attention on Ya'kov (James), he addressed them by stating, "Honored guests, family and friends. I want to thank you for coming today to join in this celebration of this momentous occasion. You have made the *bar mitzvah* (son of commandment) of my *ben* (son) Yiramiah very special, perfect and complete. At this time I would like to recognize some very special guests who have taken time from their very busy lives to celebrate with us today. First, I want to recognize Yowceph (Joseph) from the Estates of Arimathea, better known by close family members as *Qatan Yow* (little Joe), the best friend of my deceased father Chizqiy Aer (Charles Ayers). He is here today with his three-year old son, Yowcephus. I also want to recognize two brothers who have made today special, Ya'kov ben Zabdiy (James son of Zebedee) and Yowchanan ben Zabdiy (John son of Zebedee). As you know Ya'kov is the leader of the church here in Yruwshalaim (Jerusalem) of those who believe that Yahusha is the risen Machiach (Anointed or Messiah) of Yahuah and Yowchanan the beloved disciple of Yahusha who was the instructor for my son, Yiramiah (Jerry)."

Ya'kov Aer (James Ayers) continued, "Now may Yahuah bless the food and drink we are about to consume, may it nourish our bodies and may the festivities of this occasion be cherished memories in your hearts as you celebrate with us the *bar mitzvah* (son of commandment) of our son Yiramiah Aer (Jerry Ayers." Yiramiah clapped his hands and shouted, "Let's eat!" This brought a roar of laughter from the crowd of guests as all made their way towards the vast tables of aromatic cuisine. The harpist once again began to strum and pluck the strings of the harp sending waves of soothing melodious notes to the ears of all those in attendance which helped to keep the meal time chatter and laughter to a low pitch.

Following the completion of the tantalizing meal of fine morsels, it was time for the *bar mitzvah* speech of Yiramiah. According to Hebrew tradition it was customary for the *bar mitzvah* boy to deliver a speech after the reception. The speech usually consisted of a thought from the Torah portion read during his ceremony at the synagogue, which the young man will apply in some way to his own life. The purpose of the speech is to encourage the *bar mitzvah* (son of commandment) boy in the Hebrew tradition of sharing the Torah he has learned with others. The crowd of guests became quiet as Yiramiah stood up and began to deliver his speech.

Yiramiah (Jerry) began, "As most of you know my Torah reading came from a song of Mosheh (Moses) found in the book of *Dabar* meaning 'the spoken words' (Deuteronomy) chapter thirty-two verses one through fifteen. The spoken words said that Yahuah is our Rock of refuge. To me that means that we are to hide in Him to be protected, nourished, healed and rested. As our Rock He is unmovable, can't be penetrated by our enemies and is long lasting. It is in the fellowship with Him that we will find truth, honor, authority, integrity, moral fidelity and security. On the other hand if we follow our wicked sinful ways of our self-serving yearning for the things of this world, then we are stupid, impious and wicked people who are not wise. However, if we remain in the refuge of His fellowship as a mighty Rock of strength that does not wain in the violent storms then we will enjoy nothing but blessings from His hand of protection, provision and promise. In the last verse, verse fifteen, Mosheh (Moses) told us that we as a nation grew fat and oily and rejected Yahuah. How have we rejected Yahuah today? Moses said that we as a nation, we as the city of Yruwshalaim (Jerusalem), we through the members of the Sanhedrin priesthood rejected Yahuah by despising with wicked disgrace the Rock of His *Yahusha* (Salvation). That's right, we stood by silent as the members of our priesthood crucified Yahusha HaMachiach (the Anointed or Messiah)."

These words of truth made several guests uncomfortable and they began to groan and grumble. Yiramiah raised his hands to quiet them down and said, "Guests, family and friends these are not the words of Yiramiah Aer (Jerry Ayers). These are the very words from the Torah given to us by Mosheh (Moses) from Yahuah Himself. If you condemn me for these words then you are condemning the very words of Yahuah!" This response from Yiramiah brought spontaneous clapping and cheering as some of those who were offended began to exit the courtyard.

Yiramiah then continued, "It is at this time that I would like to thank the best parents a *bar mitzvah* (son of commandment) could ever have and a special thank you to all the family members and wonderful friends who have come out to make this a very special day of celebration for me. Now it is time to reveal my *Mitzvah* project to you. All the funds raised for this project will go to feed the malnourished, neglected and starving children living on the streets of the Lower City of Yruwshalaim (Jerusalem). Now please enjoy the celebration of this evening."

Then members of the crowd of guests began to shower Yiramiah with morsels of candy symbolic of sweet blessings from above. In the meantime they began to sing and dance to *'Mazal tov un simon tov'* (Good Luck and Good Signs) played on instruments of flutes, tambourines, and strings. *'Siman tov u'mazal tov, mazal tov v'siman tov, siman tov u'mazal tov, mazel tov v'siman tov, y'hey lanu? Y'hey lanu, y'hey lanu, U'l'khol Yisra'Yah, y'hey lanu, y'hey lanu, u'l'khol Yisrah'Yah* (Good signs and good luck, good luck and good signs, good signs and good luck, good luck and good signs. Good signs and good luck, good luck and good signs for us. For us, for us all and all of Israel. For us and all of Israel.) This song got the party really rocking as the musical instruments burst into the song of *Hava Nagila* (Let's

Rejoice). Everyone began to sing, clap their hands and circle dance. *Hava nagila, hava nagila, hava nigila ve-nismeha. Hava neranenah, hava neranenah, hava neranenah ve-nismeha. Uru, uru ahim! Uru ahim be-lev sameah. Uru ahim, uru ahim! Be-lev sameah* (Let's rejoice, let's rejoice, let's rejoice and be happy. Let's sing, let's sing, let's sing and be happy. Awake, awake, my brothers! Awake my brothers with a happy heart. Awake, my brothers, awake, my brothers! With a happy heart).

11

The next year in 41 A.D., the numbers of those who believed that Yahusha was the Son of Yahuah and HaMachiach (Anointed or Messiah) began to grow very rapidly causing political dissention in the ranks of the Sanhedrin and power of the priesthood. The political party of the Pharisees waned as they were losing favor and power of influence over the Roman authority placed on the throne of the palace of Pilate. These events sent shock waves among the Temple elite and turned the political party of the Sadducees into a party of ravenous wolves seeking to devour the prey of the wounded party of the Pharisees. All the *Kohen* (priests) were in a state of mistrust which spilled into the streets and unrest began to set in with the common Hebrew which the unrest unnerved the Romans.

The Sanhedrin called for an election and during the debate Jonathan ben (son of) Ananus gave a very wordy speech about how his family over the years prospered the members of the Sanhedrin and how Temple revenue had increased. He also reminded them that several members would not have a seat on the Sanhedrin if it was not for the influence of his father Ananus. In addition Jonathan reminded them that it was his family some eleven years ago that got rid of that false prophet Yahusha through the manipulation of their power with the local Roman authorities. This brought about a screaming debate with the Sadducees stating the fact that His sect still existed and grew stronger each and every day because of the mishandling of the matter by Caiaphas and his father Ananus. Even Sha'uwl (Paul) a proclaimed

Pharisee of all Pharisees had now joined the new sect preaching to the Gentiles. A call for a vote quickly came before the Sanhedrin and enough ultra-conservative Pharisees jumped party lines to give Simon Cantatheras ben Boethus, an outspoken Sadducee, the crown of HaGadowl Kohen (the High Priest) toppling the power structure that had been in control for many decades.

Power struggles were not just exclusive to the Temple in the Great City of Yruwshalaim (Jerusalem). The putrid smoldering pot of Satan had once again been stoked and its smoke of death and destruction boiled out of the rancid pot of Hades. Satan with the power of a great dragon inhaled a deep breath and blew with all his might into the smoke causing it to drift with great speed like a boiling storm towards Rome. He once again released the great Vulture of Death taking with it many demonic minions to do the bidding of the dark lord Satan. In January of 41 A.D. darkness clouded over the sun by day and the moon by night. The Roman people prayed to their false gods with all their might but the sound of their breath fell upon deaf ears. Sickness and disease spread like wildfire through the work of the demonic minions and the Vulture of Death just hovered overhead flapping its giant black dragon-like wings just waiting to sink its long sharp talons of poison into the flesh of any human being that even dared to cough. The feeding upon human flesh incited the black Vulture of Death to bellow out its eerie and bone-chilling screams as it swooped down upon its next helpless victim.

In early January of 41 A.D. Caesar Caligula announced to those who he had been the harshest with past four years including the entire Roman Senate, the nobility and to the equestran order of Rome that he intended to leave Rome permanently at the end of the month and move to Alexandria Egypt where he would be worshiped as a living god. This announcement escalated the feud between

Caesar Caligula and the political elite of Rome. The prospect of losing its emperor and thus its political power was the final straw for many in the political circles because such a move would have left both the Senate and the Praetorian Guard powerless to stop the repression and debauchery of Caesar Caligula.

On January 24, 41 A.D. the massive Vulture of Death opened the talons on its feet wide open and pierced any human flesh that could be caught within the circles of the Roman Palace because Satan was the only god to be worshiped, not some second-rate Roman Caesar. Even though early assassination plots to kill Caesar Caligula failed to the disappointment of the black Vulture, eventually officers within the Praetorian Guard led by Cassius Chaerea succeeded in murdering Emperor Caligula. This plot involved many in the Roman Senate, the army and even the equestrian order. With the taste of fresh human blood on the tongue of the Vulture of Death it screamed for more sending the demonic minions of Satan scrambling throughout the palace. The assassins uncomfortable with lingering imperial support, sought out and stabbed Caligula's wife, Caesonia and then killed their young daughter, Julia Drusilla by smashing her head against a wall repeatedly.

The Praetorian Guard then made fifty-one year old Claudius, the uncle of Caligula, as the new Caesar of Rome. This move infuriated the Roman Senate because they wanted to reinstate the Roman Republic giving them all the power instead of the throne of Rome held strongly by the Imperial Families since the time of Julius Caesar. Nineteen days later on February 12th, Claudius sired a son by Valeria Massalina, the Empress Consort of Rome and named him Tiberius Claudius Caesar Britannicus.

The now fourteen-year old Yiramiah Aer (Jerry Ayers) came sprinting through the open courtyard of his house just huffing, puffing and screaming at the top of his lungs, *"Ab, ab* (Father, Father) where are you?" He ran to the fan makers shop in the back and continued to frantically search for his father who had seemed to allude him at every turn. *"Ab, ab* (Father, father)" he continued to shout so loud that even the next door neighbors and the people across the street came running to the distress call of Yiramiah. Ya'kov Aer (James Ayers) who had gone to the front door instead of the back door, opened it up to find most of the neighborhood standing in the front courtyard of his home. Then in a flash Yiramiah came running full speed through the back of the house and tripped on the throw rug at the front door and went rolling out of the house head over heels coming to a screeching halt in the front lawn. Ya'kov shook his head and said, "What is wrong with you boy? Have you lost your mind?!" Yiramiah laid sprawled out on the front lawn and after bringing himself to his knees, he sat there for a moment panting like a ravenous dog trying to catch his breath.

One of the neighbors closest to where Yiramiah had come to an abrupt stop after tumbling out of the front door help him to his feet and brushed the dirt off his backside and the grass out of his curly black hair. Yiramiah grabbed a hold of his father's hand and said, "I have some big, big news!" Ya'kov curious about all this ruckus and fuss asked, "Well, what is it?" Yiramiah answered, "You will not believe it, but it is happening. I heard it with my own two ears as plain as day. You just won't believe it!" Ya'kov not getting a straight answer, became frustrated and asked, "What won't I believe? What has happened? Are you in trouble with the Romans? Did you try to debate the priests again about Yahusha?" Yiramiah raised his hands and shook his head back and forth like a reed in the blowing wind, "No, no, no. Nothing like that father. You just won't believe it!" Ya'kov and the neighbors just about had all the suspense that they could stand so Ya'kov calmly said, "Yiramiah take a deep breath and just start from the beginning."

Then Yiramiah began the anticipated narrative as everyone had their eyes and ears fixed upon the young lad, "Daniy'el (Daniel), Miykayhuw (Micah) and I were playing kick ball in the open square by the Temple when Daniy'el kicked the ball too hard it went into some shrubbery by the bridge south of the Xystrus Market. So we all chased the ball and when we found it, it laid not too far from ex-*Gadowl Kohen* (High Priest) Jonathan ben Ananus talking to his brother *Kohen* (Priest) Matthias ben Ananus on the other side of the wall in loud whispers. We did not intend on listening through the garden wall behind the shrubbery but we heard the words 'new Caesar, new king and new priest' so we quietly hid behind the shrubbery and peeked through the cracks in the wall. Then we heard it. Caesar Caligula has been assassinated, Claudius is now Caesar and he had given Herod Agrippa I the territory of Yhuwdah (Judah) to be king and Herod Agrippa I has promised to help restore the Pharisee Sect to the office of *HaGadowl Kohen* (the High Priest). What does all this mean?"

Ya'kov and the small crowd of neighbors were stunned in silence and just stood there for a brief moment but it seemed like an eternity as time stood still. Then one of the neighbors let out, "*Oy Vey! Agrippa melek!* (Oh, no! Agrippa King?)" Then Ya'kov dismissed the small crowd and encouraged them to return immediately to their own homes and discuss this with their families. However, he reminded them to treat this just as a rumor because it was a conversation heard through a wall by three excitable teenage boys who should not have been eavesdropping. What they just heard was to be treated with extreme caution yet at the same time be considered very serious news especially to those who were believers in Yahusha as *HaMachaich* (the Anointed or Messiah). As soon as the crowd had dispersed, Ya'kov instructed Yiramiah (Jerry) to go get Kepha (Peter), Yowchanan (John) and his brother Ya'kov (James) and bring them to the house without delay and that when they arrived he would explain everything to Yiramiah in detail.

Yiramiah quickly did what his father had instructed and when the four of them arrived, they were quickly and quietly ushered into the privacy of a secluded back room of the house with the mother of Yiramiah watching the only entrance of access to the room. They all sat down on the sitting pillows and Ya'kov looked at each one of them while gently stroking his beard. He then asked Yiramiah to repeat what he had heard to the three disciples of Yahusha and the three disciples were slightly taken aback. Then Yiramiah asked, "Father why is everyone so concerned and what does this news mean?"

Therefore, Ya'kov (James) the father of Yiramiah began to explain, "You see son, a long time ago before you were born, Herod Agrippa was born into the powerful Herod family in eleven (11) B.C. He was the grandson of Herod the Great and the son of Aristobulus IV. His given name was Marcus Julius Agrippa, so named in honor of the Roman statesman Marcus Vispanius Agrippa. Today he is referred to as 'Agrippa the Great' because he also has a son, just a year younger than you also named Marcus Julius Agrippa but he is known as Herod Agrippa II. After the father of Herod Agrippa I, Aristobulus IV, was murdered he was sent by Herod the Great to the imperial court in Rome. There, then Caesar Tiberius conceived a great affection for him and had him educated alongside his son Drusus. It was during those times that Drusus and young Claudius befriended him. After the sudden death of Drusus, Herod Agrippa I, who had been recklessly extravagant and was deeply in debt, was obliged to leave Rome, fleeing to the fortress of Malatha in Idumaea (country of Edom, modern southern Jordan). Remember son, that Edom 'meaning red' was originally founded by *Esav* (Esau) the oldest son of *Yitschaq* (Isaac) who had sold his birthright to our patriarch Yisra'Yah (Israel) for some red bean stew."

After a brief pause Ya'kov (James) continued, "Anyway it was at the fortress of Malatha where Herod Agrippa I contemplated suicide. After a brief seclusion, through the mediation of his wife Cyprus and his sister Herodias, Herod Agrippa I was given a large sum of money by his brother-in-law and uncle, the husband of Herodias, Herod Antipas also known as Herod Antipater, the Tetrarch of Galilee and Perea and was allowed to take up residence in the city of Tiberius, located on the shores of Galilee. He was given the rank of *aedile* and was responsible for the maintenance of public buildings, regulation of public festivals and to enforce public order for a small yearly income. Then he quarreled with Herod Antipas and fled to Flaccus the proconsul of Syria. Soon afterwards he was convicted, through information of his brother Aristobulus V of having received a bribe from certain high ranking people in the city of Damascus that wished to purchase his influence with the proconsul and was again compelled to flee for his life. However, he was arrested as he was about to sail for Italy, for a sum of money which he owed to the treasury of Caesar. He was very crafty and made his escape and reached Alexandria, Egypt where his wife succeeded in procuring a large supply of money from Alexander the Alabarch. He then set sail and landed at Puteoli, a township of Naples, Italy. It was here that he was favorably received by Caesar Tiberius, who entrusted him with the education of his grandson Tiberius Gemellus and he rekindled the friendship with Caligula. One day Herod Agrippa I was overheard by his freedman Eutyches expressing a wish for the death of Caesar Tiberus and the advancement of Caligula, and for this he was cast into prison."

Ya'kov stopped for a moment to address his son Yiramiah, "Son, I tell you this so that you fully realize the moral character of Herod Agrippa I. I hope that you can see that he is a very treacherous and greedy man who will do anything to better himself financially and politically. Even to the extent of having enough power and influence to be involved with the plotting of an assassination of a Roman Caesar." "I am beginning to understand, father," replied young Yiramiah (Jerry). Then Kepha (Peter) spoke up, "Yiramiah, listen closely to your father because what he says is true." Yiramiah answered, "*Ken, ken* (Yes, yes)."

Ya'kov took a deep breath and continued to instruct Yiramiah, "Then following the death of Caesar Tiberus four years ago, when you were ten years old, of course the friend of Herod Agrippa I, Caligula was made Caesar. Thus Herod Agrippa I, was set free from prison and made king over the territories of Gaulanitis (area east of the Sea of Galilee modern Golan Heights Israel), Auranitis (a volcanic plateau called Horan modern SW Syria), Batanaea (Bashan NE of Jordon River modern Northern Jordan) and Trachonitis (southern Syria), which his uncle Philip the Tetrarch had held plus the territory of Abila (mountain region of Damascus, Syria also called Abilene)."

"Not only was Herod Agrippa I given these territories to rule as king but he was also awarded the *ornamenta praetoria* (golden ornament or neckless of a magistrate) and could use the title of *amicus caesaris* (friend of Caesar). Caligula also presented him with a gold chain equal in weight to the iron one he had worn in prison, which two years ago Herod Agrippa I dedicated to the Temple of Yruwshalaim (Jerusalem) when he returned briefly to visit his ancestral homeland. At that time when he returned to Rome and brought about the banishment of his uncle, Herod Antipater, he was granted the Tetrarchy of his uncle consisting of the territories of Galilee and Peraea. It has even been rumored that Herod Agrippa I was involved behind the scenes of the assassination of his dear friend Caligula so that Claudius could become Caesar."

Then Ya'kov (James) took his eyes of his son Yiramiah (Jerry) and addressed everyone in the secluded room, "My dear spiritual brothers Kepha (Peter), Ya'kov (James) and Yowchanan (John) and of course my son Yiramiah. What I am about to say must be kept silent and a secret until we learn if the news that Yiramiah heard was true or not. You see if it is true and this treacherous man has been made our king, who has direct ties to the throne in Rome then our lives are in danger. Herod Agrippa I has a long family history of hating the followers of Yahusha ever since his uncle Herod Antipas had Yowchanan Baptista (John the Baptist) beheaded. If he has been made our king then the Pharisee sect will once again control the Temple with the family of Ananus dictating policy. As you all know it was during the tenure of the Ananus family that demanded the crucifixion of Yahusha our *Machiach* (Anointed or Messiah). Now armed with the power of the Temple, the power of the Territory and the power of the Throne in Rome, the Ananus Priesthood will seek out to destroy all the believers of Yahusha. Now depart and pray my brothers but do not warn anyone else until we get official notification from Rome."

The three disciples departed the home of the fan maker Ya'kov Aer (James Ayers) and returned to their place of gathering. One week later a public crier from Rome galloped into the city escorted by Roman Calvary and proceeded to the large open air public square to read the message from the rolled up parchment. After the summoned and curious crowd stopped milling and became somewhat silent he began his announcement, "Hear ye, hear ye, servants of the great throne of Rome. Tiberius Claudius Caesar Augustus Germanicus has been made Emperor Caesar over the Roman Empire. Your loyalty is demanded to yield in humility to him or your life will be forfeit if any insurrection against the throne or him is found. In addition Caesar Claudius has given kingship over this territory known as Yhuwdah (Judah) to his long-time friend and ally Herod Agrippa I. You are commanded to honor and obey the commands of your new king as well as the financial requests from Caesar in Rome. Any dissention or insurrection against your new king will be considered dissention or insurrection against the throne in Rome itself and will be punishable by death of crucifixion on a cross. This order is by my hand Caesar Claudius, Emperor of Rome."

With the addition of the territories of Judah and Samaria, Caesar Claudius also made King Herod Agrippa I as *ornamenta consularia* and at his request have the kingdoms of Chalcis and Lebanon given to Agrippa's brother Herod of Chalcis. Therefore, King Herod Agrippa I became one of the most powerful kings of the entire East. His domain more or less equaled that which was held by his grandfather Herod the Great.

Two years later in 43 A.D. the infighting within the Sanhedrin between the Pharisees and the Sadducees had produced so much hatred, discontent, greed and vengeance that the loud grumbling from the Temple in Yruwshalaim (Jerusalem) caught the ears of the blood-thirsty Vulture of Death as it continued to circle over the throne in Rome. The grumbling between the Pharisees and the Sadducees, the envy that was held by the *Kohen* (Priests) against the followers of Yahusha *HaMachiach* (the Anointed or Messiah) and the kingship of a pro-Pharisee and an attitude of anti-follower of Yahusha in King Herod Agrippa I brought a blood-curdling and bone chilling scream from deep within the depths of evil. Satan sent the pitch black cauldron into a full boil of thick rancid choking smoke billowing upwards towards the location of the venomous murdering massive Vulture of Death hovering above Rome spreading death and disease through the minions of the dark lord Satan.

When the Vulture of Death heard the call of his dark lord Satan, it let out an eerie high-pitched bellow in response. Then the great dragon of the air released a pair of black swirling whirlwinds from its nasty nostrils tainted with the smell of death and destruction. They were headed full steam towards the Great City of Yruwshalaim (Jerusalem). Instantly, four magnificent warrior messengers of Yahuah traveled at the speed of the Great Light to intercept the two dark and evil whirlwinds of death and destruction. The two powerful and giant forces of good and evil collided in the atmosphere making the sound of a great thunder over the Sea of Galilee. The first two warrior messengers of Yahuah grabbed the head and tail of one of the swirling whirlwinds and with the mighty unstoppable power of the Sacred Breath rode the rotation in the opposite direction making the whirlwind choke itself out and disappear into thin air. The second pair of warrior messengers intercepted the second whirlwind just outside the walls of Yruwshalaim (Jerusalem) which was now twisting and dancing in all directions in an attempt to keep from being contained. The whirlwind dipped deep into the atmosphere causing one of the two warriors to dive rapidly but not before the whirlwind had touched off a few storm clouds and a brief rain shower. Finally, the second whirlwind was fully contained and rendered powerless and dissipated into thin air.

Even though the warrior messengers of Yahuah had prevented the evil whirlwinds of death and destruction from causing tremendous havoc upon the residents of the Great City of Yruwshalaim (Jerusalem), the brief rain shower pelted the streets with the contaminated poison from the nostrils of the Vulture of Death. Though only brief and miniscule it was enough potent poison to inflame thoughts of murder and hatred paving the way for the massive black winged Vulture of Death to once again occupy the air over the Great City of Yruwshalaim (Jerusalem). The obedient minions of Satan followed the evil black dragon of the air ready for the demonic cruelty they would inflict upon the unaware and unsuspecting people of the Great City.

Meanwhile, in the city of Berytus (modern day Beirut, Lebanon), King Herod Agrippa I was busy building a theatre and amphitheater, baths and porticoes. He was equally generous in the cities of Sebaste, Heliopolis and Caesarea. Agrippa began the building of the third and outer wall of the Great City of Yruwshalaim (Jerusalem) but the suspicions he had of the intervention of Caesar Claudius prevented him from finishing the fortification which he had begun. His friendship was courted by many of the neighboring kings and rulers, some of whom he housed in Tiberius, which also caused Caesar Claudius some displeasure.

With the political influence and support of King Herod Agrippa I, the Pharisees maneuvered an election that year in 43 A.D. Just before the election two powerbroker Sadducees were found dead and a third one missing leaving the Sanhedrin in full control with the Pharisee Sect. When the election results were tallied the result was that the sons of Ananus once again narrowly regained the position of *HaGadowl Kohen* (the High Priest). Matthias ben Ananus was elected to be in command of the Temple and religious order of the Hebrew people. The venomous and contagious poison that had hit the pavement of the streets of Yruwshalaim (Jerusalem) from that brief rain shower began to take effect.

Immediately upon taking the office of *HaGadowl Kohen* (the High Priest) Matthias ben Ananus vigorously sought to silence and punish those who followed the teaching of Yahusha. Opposing him were the Sadducees, who do not believe in resurrection of the dead, argued why worry about a dead man that the Temple had more important matters to contend with. They also pointed out that the Pharisees could not be trusted because even one of their brightest and most zealous Pharisees Sha'uwl (Paul) had deserted their sect and had become a follower of this dead man called Yahusha. After a few months of heated debate, hurling of insults, and even hatred for their fellow *Kohen (*Priests) another election was demanded in order to stop the unrest. This time however, Sadducee Elioneus ben Simon Cantatheras the son of the previous disposed *HaGadowl Kohen* (the High Priest) carried the votes by one. This made the Ananus family and leading Pharisees scramble to King Herod Agrippa I for help once again and this time to bring about the power of his Kingship to eliminate the movement of the followers of Yahusha in his territory, which was vast and sprawling.

Although things were in disarray among the religious elite in Yruwshalaim (Jerusalem), exciting news was taking place elsewhere. Those followers of Yahusha who were distributed throughout foreign lands because of the pressure that came into being over Stephanos (Steven) traveled to the palm country of Phoinike (Palestine) and the Island of Kupros (Cyprus) and the town of Antiocheia (Antioch) in Syria, talking to not even one except only the Yhuwdiy (Hebrews). But some of them were men, *Kuprios* from the Island of Cyprus and *Kurenaioas* from the town of Cyrene, Libya who entered to the town of Antioch, Syria to talk to the *Hellenistes* (Greek speaking Hebrews) announcing the good news of the Gospel of Yahusha the Anointed Messiah of Yahweh. The Messiah's hand was with them and a large number had faith to entrust their spiritual well-being to the Messiah and reverted to Yahusha.

This topic was heard in the ears of the congregation in Yruwshalaim (Jerusalem) with respect to them and they sent forth on a mission Bar-abiy (Barnabas) to travel to Antiocheia (Antioch, Syria). When he arrived and saw the graciousness of Yahuah and became cheerful and happy and invoked with all intention to expose his heart of feelings and thought to remain near the Messiah because he was a good man and covered completely over with the Sacred Breath and of moral convection of the truth of Yahuah and reliance upon the Messiah for salvation. An ample amount and fit in character of a throng of rabble was placed additional to the Messiah during his stay.

Then Bar-nbiy (Barnabas) issued forth to the town of Tarsos (Tarsas) Syria to search out Sha'uwl (Paul) and finding him he led him to the town of Antiocheia (Antioch, Syria). It came into being a whole year that Sha'uwl (Paul) and Bar-nbiy (Barnabas) were convened together in the congregation and taught an ample amount of a throng of rabble and at first, the pupils of Antiocheia (Antioch, Syria) bore the title of Messiah Followers.

In those days inspired prophets came down from Yruwshalaim (Jerusalem) to Antiocheia (Antioch Syria). One of them stood up by the name of Chagab (Agabus) meaning 'locust' indicated through the Sacred Breath that a great scarcity of food and destitution was about to be all over the Roman Empire, which also came into being during the time of Caesar Claudius. The pupils as many that possessed money in Antocheia (Antioch, Syria) appointed each of them for aid to bestow to those brothers in Yhuwdah (Judea). They gave very generously and sent out on a mission to the senior members of the *Knesi'Yah* (Gathered People of Yahuah) following the teachings of

Yahusha in the Great City of Yruwshalaim (Jerusalem) through the hands of Sha'uwl (Paul) and Bar-niby (Barnabas) with the generous gift. Sha'uwl and Bar-niby returned to Antiocheia (Antioch, Syria) taking with them Yowchanan (John) also called Mark, the cousin of Bar-niby and ministered there.

When the Pharisees found out about the gift from the city of Antocheia (Antioch, Syria) for the *Knesi'Yah* (Gathered People of Yahuah) who followed the teachings of Yahusha as their *HaMachiach* (the Anointed or Messiah) they became livid with envy. Ananus had recently died that year, so his five sons and his son-in-law Caiaphas met privately with King Herod Agrippa I and complained about the recent activity of the Yahusha *Knesi'Yah* (Gathered People of Yahuah). They pleaded with him to return to Yruwshalaim (Jerusalem) to govern it and help once again to permanently return the power of the Temple back to their family. Therefore,...

12

King Herod Agrippa I returned to territory of Yhuwdah (Judea) to the Great City of Yruwshalaim (Jerusalem) in 44 A.D. He governed it to the satisfaction of the Yhuwdiy (Hebrews) and his zeal, private and public, for Judaism was noted by both sects of the *Kohen* (Priests) the Pharisee and Sadducee alike. They remembered that it was his influence in 41 A.D. at the risk of his own life as he passionately interceded on the behalf of the Yhuwdiy (Hebrews) with Caesar Caligula against the idea of the emperor attempting to set up his statue in the Temple at Yruwshalaim (Jerusalem) shortly before his assassination. It was through the efforts of Herod Agrippa I that bore fruit and persuaded Caesar Caligula to rescind his order thus preventing the desecration of the Temple. They also remembered the very valuable donation of the golden chain presented to him by Caesar Claudius equaling the weight of the chain that Agrippa bore while in prison. He loved the Yhuwdiy (Hebrews) and they loved him as king, yet he passionately hated and disdained Yahusha *Knesi'Yah* (Yahusha's Gathered People of Yahuah). This passion of deep evil hatred helped fuel the fires of the Pharisee Sect and the Priestly family of Ananus.

The first order of business was to get the Temple leadership under control so that there would be a sense of stability from the Priesthood not only for the sake of the Temple but also for the trust of the common Yhuwdiy (Hebrew) against the fast growing numbers of Yahusha *Knesi'Yah* (Yahusha's Gathered People of Yahuah). Therefore, King Herod Agrippa I ordered a new election in the winter of 44

A.D. and the newly elected *HaGadowl Kohen* (the High Priest) was Jonathan ben Ananus restoring the Temple leadership back to the Pharisees and to the Ananus family.

The second order of business was more sinister by King Herod Agrippa I. He ordered a raid on the Yahusha *Knesi'Yah* (Yahusha's Gathered People of Yahuah). The King was granted permission by Rome under the guise of squelching a coup against the Roman Throne of Caesar Claudius and sent sixty armed Roman soldiers in riot gear and arrested over one hundred (100) men and women loyal to the Yahusha *Knesi'Yah* (Yahusha's Gathered People of Yahuah). Among them was Ya'kov ben Zabdiiy (James son of Zebedee) the brother of Yowchanan (John) and the first cousin of *Yahusha HaMachiach* (Yahusha the Anointed or Messiah). Ya'kov was removed from the Great City of Yruwshalaim (Jerusalem) and was taken to Palestine. The next morning King Herod Agrippa I had Ya'kov beheaded with a sword knowing that Ya'kov was a strong leader of Yahusha *Knesi'Yah* (Yahusha's Gathered People of Yahuah). The Roman officer who guarded Ya'kov watched amazed as Ya'kov defended his faith at his trial. Later, the Roman officer walked beside Ya'kov to the place of execution. The Roman officer overcame by conviction confessed and declared his new faith to King Herod Agrippa I. Then he knelt beside Ya'kov to accept beheading as a new Messiah Follower.

When King Herod Agrippa I saw that the murder of Ya'kov pleased the Yhuwdiy (Hebrews) specifically the Pharisee Sect, he sent out legions of Roman soldiers to hunt down and arrest Kepha (Peter). These days were following the *Pesach* (Passover) during the *Chag Ha Matstsah Lechem* (Festival of the Unleavened Bread) when Kepha (Peter) was hunted and officially arrested. He was placed in a guarded place with four squads of four Roman soldiers (sixteen men total) to guard him. King Herod Agrippa I was willing after the *Pesach* (Passover) celebration to lead him up to the people. Accordingly, Kepha (Peter) was guarded in the guarding place but intense prayer came into being by the congregation to Yahuah with respect to him. When King Herod Agrippa I was about to lead him out by night and Kepha (Peter) was sleeping in a deep slumber between two Roman warriors, having been bound with two fetters and manacles. Also, watchful sentries were in front of the prison door guarding the guarded place. Then all of a sudden, a messenger angel from Yahuah stood to be present and a light beamed with a radiate brilliancy in the jail. Then knocking gently the side of Kepha (Peter) he woke him from his sleep expressing, "Stand up in haste!" Immediately the fetters and manacled dropped away from his hands and feet. The messenger angel said to him, "Gird on your clothes all around and fasten your belt and put on your sandals!" Kepha (Peter) did as the messenger angel had instructed him to do. Then the messenger angel said in a deep voice, "Throw on your outer dress and accompany me." After issuing out he accompanied the messenger angel and Kepha (Peter) did not know that this was truly coming into being through the messenger angel. He thought he was only seeing a supernatural spectacle. After traveling through the first guard and then the second, they came to the gate made of iron leading one to the city, which of itself was opened up to them. After issuing out of the iron-gate they preceded to one alley and the messenger angel at once issued forth from him. Yahuah did this to make Kepha (Peter) aware and understand all of the evil infliction that was to be anticipated from the people of the Yhuwdiy (Hebrews) towards him. The next day, King Herod Agrippa I searched for him and did not find him. Therefore, he investigated the matter by interrogating the watching sentries and ordered for them to be taken away for execution.

This matter was so troubling to King Herod Agrippa I, that he left Yruwshalaim (Jerusalem) and traveled to the city of Kaisereia (Caesarea) and remained there. King Herod Agrippa I was bitterly angry with the towns of Turios and Sidonios (Tyre and Sidon). Representatives from the two towns came near to him with one mind and one passion and convinced the officer of King Herod Agrippa I named Blastos meaning 'sprout' the one in charge of the bedroom of the sovereign and they asked for peace because they got a stiffen of food from the territory of King Herod Agrippa I. Thus on an arranged and stated day, King Herod Agrippa I invested with clothing a regal dress and sat on the step of the rostrum and addressed a public assembly to them. The public bound together socially and was exclaiming, "A voice of a god and not of a human being" You see the outer dress of King Herod was of pure silver and with the sunrise rays bouncing off the silver of the outer garment he appeared to be radiate. King Herod Agrippa I did not refute or dispute what the crowd was yelling but received their acclamation with pride. Then a messenger angel of Yahuah knocked him down fatally because he did not give the glory to Yahuah. Therefore, he became very ill and was eaten alive in his guts by a disease of maggot worms and died five days later.

King Herod Agrippa I was a cruel, heartless, treacherous, murderous and contemptuous man who connived against the most powerful men of the known world at that time. His fortunes amassed a mere twelve million drachamae equaling 1.9 million United States dollars, ($1,900,000.00). He was a brilliant carbon copy of his grandfather Herod the Great without the mental disorders. King Herod Agrippa I died at the age of fifty-four years old. His vast empire and debts were passed on to his only son, Herod Agrippa II at the age of seventeen with the blessings of Caesar Claudius.

However, since Herod Agrippa II was only seventeen years old he was educated at the court of Caesar Claudius. Caesar Claudius therefore kept him at Rome and sent Cuspius Fadus as procurator for the Roman province of Yhuwdah (Judea). While at Rome, Herod Agrippa II voiced his support for the support of the Yhuwdiy (Hebrews) to Caesar Claudius and repeated the contempt of his father for the Yahusha *Knesi'Yah* (Yahusha's Gathered People of Yahuah) and the Samaritans. While he had the ear of Caesar Claudius, he also expressed his displeasure for the procurator of the province of Yhuwdah (Judea), Ventidius Cumanus, who was thought to have been the cause of several disturbances there.

HaGadowl Kohen (The High Priest) Jonathan ben Ananus became very ill so his best friend and ally Pharisee Josephus ben Camydus was given the priestly turban to wear. An election was not held due to an executive order from King Herod Agrippa II because of the mourning period of his father King Herod Agrippa I. Josephus ben Camydus was more aggressive than Jonathan ben Ananus and with the full authority of King Herod Agrippa II, he used his position in the Temple to hunt down and persecute members of the Yahusha *Knesi'Yah* (Yahusha's Gathered People of Yahuah).

Two years passed by in a relative quiet fashion. This year of 46 A.D. was a landmark year. First of all in the early winter an election was held for the position of *Gadowl Kohen* (High Priest) and once again the Pharisee sect maintained a firm grip on the government of the Temple by electing Ananias ben Nebedeus a devoted member of the Pharisees. Also, that year Ya'kov (James), the half-brother of Yahusha *HaMachiach* (the Anointed or Messiah) wrote the first book to be included in the New Testament, which was the Book of James. The minions of Satan continued to do their dastardly deeds as several plots to kill Caesar Claudius began their planning stages.

In the fall of 46 A.D. Sha'uwl (Paul) began his first missionary trip calling it "Let the Light Shine". You see in the town of Antioceua (Antioch, Syria) among the congregation of the Yahusha *Knesi'Yah* (Yahusha's Gathered People of Yahuah) were inspired prophets and instructors. Both Bar-nbiy (Barnabas) and Shim'own (Simon) who was called Niger meaning 'black' and Luokios (Lucius) meaning 'illuminative' the one from Cyrene Libya and Manean who had been brought up with Herod the Tetrarch and also Sha'uwl (Paul). They were being public servants doing charitable functions to Yahuah and religiously abstaining from food when the Sacred Breath said, "Now then appoint to Me both Bar-nbiy (Barnabas) and Sha'uwl (Paul) for the work to which I have summoned them. They are to preach the Good News of the Gospel of Yahusha to many of the spiritually lost Yhuwdiy (Hebrews) and Gentiles in many strange territories. Go to the first city that I will tell you and preach the Good News of the Gospel of Yahusha until I come to you and tell you where to go next. Today, Sha'uwl (Paul) and Bar-nbiy (Barnabas), I instruct you to go to the port city of Seleukeia (Seleucia) and wait for a boat there leaving early tomorrow morning to cross The Great Sea (Mediterranean Sea) to the city of Salamis on the Island of Kupros (Cyrpus)."

Bar-nbiy (Barnabas) became excited and exclaimed, "Great, a trip, I love to travel don't you Sha'uwl (Paul)?" As he continued to look at Sha'uwl (Paul) for an answer, he began clapping his hands together. Sha'uwl (Paul) replied, "Bar-nbiy (Barnabas) to be honest I really don't like boats. However, I am excited to serve our Messiah, Yahusha the Son of Yahuah." Then Sha'uwl (Paul) asked the Sacred Breath, "Is there any further instructions that you need to give us?" The Sacred Breath said in a deep tone like thunder, "Yes. There have been many reports of the Pharisees stirring up trouble in the regions that I will be sending you. You must beware of their sharp lying tongues and their deadly hands because Satan has commanded his minion demons to influence the religious leaders to increase their persecution of the Yahusha *Knesi'Yah* (Yahusha's Gathered People of Yahuah)." Then the Sacred Breath disappeared. Niger the teacher, Luokios (Lucius), and Manean the prophet prayed and asked Yahh for travel safety for Bar-nbiy (Barnabas) and Sha'uwl (Paul). Then they all placed their hands upon them and blessed them for their obedience and bravery. Luokios (Lucius) gathered some bread, Manean gathered some dried fruit berries and Niger the teacher gathered kernels of grain and gave the collection of food to Sha'uwl (Paul) and Bar-nbiy (Barnabas). Then they said their goodbyes and sent them off on the mission trip.

When they had arrived in Seleukeia (Seleucia) they traveled through the marketplace to head towards the boat docks. It was here that Bar-nbiy (Barnabas) recognized his cousin Yowchanan (John) also known as Mark in the crowd. Yowchanan (John) Mark ran over to Bar-nbiy and greeted him with a kiss on both cheeks as was the custom in that region. Then Yowchanan (John)/Mark said, "Bar-nbiy and Sha'uwl what a surprise. What are you doing in Seleukeia (Seleucia, Syria)? I thought you were ministering in Antiocheia (Antioch Syria)! You should have sent word that you were going to visit and I would have prepared for you." Sha'uwl (Paul) responded, "Yowchanan (John) Mark we are here on business on the way to the boat docks to catch our boat." "What kind of business," questioned Yowchanan (John) Mark? Before Sha'uwl (Paul) could answer, Bar-nbiy (Barnabas) teasingly blurted out, "Oh, the very secret kind. We have been given a special mission by the Sacred Breath for Yahusha the Son of Yahuah!" "Wow, really?" exclaimed Yowchanan (John) Mark. Sha'uwl (Paul) began to laugh and said, "Yes, we are on a mission but it is not the secret kind. Bar-nbiy (Barnabas) is just teasing you my young friend." Then Bar-nbiy (Barnabas) explained that they were headed to the Island of Cyprus to preach the good news of the Gospel to the Gentiles and Yhuwdiy (Hebrews) alike. Sha'uwl (Paul) put his hand on the shoulder of Yowchanan (John) Mark and asked, "Would you like to come along with us as our helper?" "Really? You would want me to come along and help you?" excitedly asked Yowchanan (John) Mark. Bar-nbiy (Barnabas) stated, "Sure cousin if you can handle it but we had better get going or we will miss our boat."

Then the three of them hustled on down to the boat docks and paid their fare for the boat going to the Island of Cyprus. It was large wooden ship with three large white billowing sails attached to the three masts. The boat had many passengers all headed to the Island of Cyprus. Bar-nbiy (Barnabas) and Yowchanan (John)/Mark boarded the boat and settled down near the deck and prepared for a whole day's journey of sailing across the Great Mediterranean Sea. The big wooden boat creaked and rocked away from the boat dock and before they knew it they were surrounded with nothing but rocking waves with no land in sight. Sha'uwl decided to take a nap with the gentle rocking back and forth of the ship. When he woke up the sun was dipping into the sea and soon sparkling stars became a canopy above the large boat twinkling as if they were winking at the passengers.

Then it happened. The sound started low but the sound soon became a melodious choir of people singing a beautiful melody. Bar-nbiy (Barnabas) and Yowchanan (John) Mark worked their way closer to the music since they were shorter than most people and could not get a good view of the choir. However, Sha'uwl (Paul) remained where he was and shut his eyes to let the beautiful sound gently enter his ears and sooth his weary mind. Suddenly, the meditation of Sha'uwl (Paul) was interrupted by someone frantically shaking his arms. He opened his eyes and standing in front of him excitedly was Bar-nbiy (Barnabas) shouting, "Wake up! Wake up! The choir director has invited us to share the good news of the Gospel of Yahusha with the choir and their families when we reach Salamis on the Island of Cyprus. He also knows of a small congregation of Yhuwdiy (Hebrews) in the city and will make arrangements for you to speak in their midst at the synagogue." "That is wonderful news," replied Sha'uwl (Paul).

Before they knew it at the rising of the sun they could see land in the distance. "Land-a-ho" shouted the watchman to the boat captain. The captain effortlessly guided the big boat to the boat docks of the city of Salamis on the Island of Cyprus. The large wooden ship finally came to a halt and dropped its anchors making a huge splashing sound in the waters of the bay. The three missionaries said their good-byes to the choir director and the choir and then hopped down the wooden gangway to exit the boat. The city of Salamis was buzzing with many people and was very crowded. Bar-nbiy (Barnabas) saw a person who looked like as if he was a local and asked him what all the commotion was about. The man replied, "It is the annual Wine Festival when visitors to our Island can try different wines at no charge. Then there is entertainment of folk dancing and different choirs perform. You must be strangers to our quaint little Island." Yowchanan (John) Mark spoke up and said, "Yes we are. We are on a special missionary trip and need lodging." The local man rubbed his thumb and index forefinger on his chin and said, "You are in luck. My brother is an innkeeper and you could stay with him if you would like." Yowchanan (John) Mark nodded his head in affirmation, so the man led them to the inn of his brother. It was nothing fancy but it was very clean and the aroma of the food was very enticing.

The innkeeper showed them their room and that evening Sha'uwl (Paul) and Bar-nbiy (Barnabas) shared the Gospel of Yahusha with the innkeeper and his family. They believed and became members of the Yahusha *Knesi'Yah* (Yahusha's Gathered People of Yahuah). For the next several days the innkeeper led them to many homes where they shared the Good News of the Son of Yahuah. Many local people and even some Yhuwdiy (Hebrews) came to know Yahusha as *HaMachiach* (the Anointed or Messiah) as the Gospel was well received. Sha'uwl and Bar-nbiy were glad that they brought Yowchanan (John) Mark along as a helper because they were busy and sent him to look for the choir director that they had met on the boat but he and his choir could not be found. Then one of the new members of the Yahusha *Knesi'Yah* (Yahusha's Gathered People of Yahuah) informed them that the choir was summoned for a special concert at the governor's mansion. The choir had just left that morning so that they would have plenty of time to travel across the island. Therefore the choir would not be too exhausted to sing beautifully and entertain the governor and his guests.

So, Sha'uwl (Paul), Bar-nbiy (Barnabas) and Yowchanan (John) Mark gathered their few belongings and began the seventy-five mile journey across the Island of Cyprus and head to the city of Phaphos. The three missionaries traveled at double speed with hopes of catching up with the large choir and their choir director before reaching Paphos, Cyprus. After traveling four hours just before noon they caught up with the choir resting in a meadow and having lunch. Bar-nbiy (Barnabas) shouted at the choir director to get his attention and the choir director jumped up from his lunch and waved the three missionaries on in to join them. They exchanged pleasantries and after lunch they asked if they could accompany the choir to Phaphos, Cyprus as they would like to visit with the governor also. The choir director was thrilled and over the rest of the trip the three missionaries shared the good news of the Gospel with the choir director and the choir. Before they got to the city gates the message of the Gospel was graciously received by all the choir and the director and they became members of the Yahusha *Knesi'Yah* (Yahusha's Gathered People of Yahuah).

When they reached the city gates the missionaries were met by a magician who was under the influence and training of the demonic minions of the dark lord Satan. He told lies about the future and was a religious imposter and a pretend prophet. The man was an Yhuwd (Hebrew) and his name was Bar-Yahusha but the Hellenisti (Greeks) translated his name and called him Elumas (Elymas). This magician was with the Governor of Cyprus, the Roman Proconsul, who was called Sergius Paulus, a very wise man. The Governor summoned to himself Bar-nbiy (Barnabas) and Sha'uwl (Paul) and craved and demanded to hear about the Messiah of Yahuah. However, Elumas the magician and demonic wizard stood against them. For this reason his name was translated as 'wizard' plotting to distort, misinterpret and corrupt the Roman Proconsul from the moral conviction of the truth of Yahuah and the reliance upon the Messiah Yahusha for salvation.

Sha'uwl called by his Roman name Paulus being filled with the Sacred Breath gazed intently at the wizard Elumas (Elymas) and said, "Oh, completely covered of all with decoys of but for tricks and of all unscrupulous cunning, son of Satan and hatful adversary of all justification, you will not restrain or stop by distorting, misinterpreting or corrupting the straight word of Yahuah! Behold, now the hand of power of Yahuah is upon you and you will be blind, not looking at the sun until a set and proper time!" Immediately, mist and the dimness of sight like a cataract and obscure shadiness seized on him and Elumas (Elymas) the wizard walked around seeking a hand leader of a blind person. At that time, Sergius Paulus, the Roman Proconsul being the Governor saw the thing that came into being and had faith to entrust his spiritual well-being to the Messiah and was struck with astonishment at the instruction about Yahusha *HaMachiach* (the Anointed or Messiah). Therefore, he became a member of Yahusha *Knesi'Yah* (Yahusha's Gathered People of Yahuah). He set forth a decree to all the citizens of the town Phaphos, Cyprus that they should listen to the good news of the Gospel at several public meetings. After, spending a week sharing the good news of the Gospel in the city of Phaphos, the Sacred Breath instructed Sha'uwl (Paul) that they needed to board the next ship and head north across the Great Mediterranean Sea to a city called Perge meaning 'tower' of the territory of Pamphulia meaning 'every tribe' (Perga, Pamphylia what is now modern S.W. Turkey).

The next ship leaving the port was scheduled to leave late that afternoon. The three missionaries paid the fare and boarded the ship and prepared for the two-hundred mile trip across the waters of the sea. This boat was much smaller than the one that they arrived on the Island of Cyprus on and the waves tossed it about from side to side with ease. The three missionaries spent their time talking to a few of the passengers about the good news of the Gospel and a couple of them believed the Message and became members of the Yahusha *Knesi'Yah* (Yahusha's Gathered People of Yahuah). When they reached the shores of Perge, Pamphulia they saw a huge sailing ship on the docks with people filing up the wooden plank to board the ship. It was a beautiful massive ship. Bar-nbiy out of pure curiosity asked one of the dock workers where the ship was headed. The dock worker said, "Mate, this ship is carrying passengers and cargo back to the city of Yruwshalaim (Jerusalem). Its port will be at Caesarea." Bar-nbiy (Barnabas) responded, "Thank-you for the information." Yowchanan (John) Mark overheard the conversation between his cousin Bar-nbiy and the dock worker. He then suggested to Sha'uwl (Paul) and Bar-nbiy (Barnabas) that he wanted to return home. However, he thought it would be a good idea for him to journey on to the Great City of Yruwshalaim (Jerusalem) and report there to the members of the Yahusha *Knesi'Yah* (Yahusha's Gathered People of Yahuah) all the good news that happened on the Island of Cyprus. Sha'uwl (Paul) and Bar-nbiy (Barnabas) said goodbye and Yowchanan (John) Mark abandoned the mission trip.

After a brief rest in Perge, Pamphulia the Sacred Breath instructed them to travel one hundred miles north to a town called Antiocheia in the territory of Pisdia (Antioch, Pisidian modern south central Turkey). Sha'uwl (Paul) and Bar-nbiy (Barnabas) figured that the trip would take two days putting them at their destination before sundown on Friday, the beginning of the weekly Sabbath. Therefore, they decided to get some rest and check their supplies and stay overnight in Perge, Pamphulia. While at supper that evening, Sha'uwl (Paul) blessed the meal and thanked Yahuah for the blessing of a safe missionary journey. After the prayer, as they were about to eat their first bite, a gentleman with a deep baritone voice tapped Bar-nbiy (Barnabas) on the shoulder and said, "Excuse me gentlemen. I was not eavesdropping but I noticed you praying. From the accent of your speech do you happen to be Yhuwdiy (Hebrews) from around the Great City of Yruwshalaim (Jerusalem)?" Bar-nbiy (Barnabas) spoke up and replied, "Why, yes we are. How can we be of assistance to you?" The man answered, "Excuse me. I too am Yhuwdiy (Hebrew). My name is *Pashchuwr* meaning 'liberation' in Hebrew but I am called

Barytonos (Baritone) by the Greeks and *Baritono* by the Romans. My people were originally from Beyth-Lechem (Bethlehem) just outside the Great City. Now my family and I live in Antocheia, Pisidia (Antioch, Pisidian). I am here for a short visit and will be going home tomorrow."

Sha'uwl (Paul) mentally rejoiced at the continued provisions by the Sacred Breath as He prepared the way on this missionary trip. Sha'uwl (Paul) said to Baritone, "Well sir, we are traveling to Antocheia, Pisidia (Antioch, Pisidian) ourselves tomorrow!" Baritone excitedly asked, "I would love to have traveling companions on my journey home. Would you like me to be your guide and travel with you?" "That would be splendid," answered Bar-nbiy (Barnabas). Baritone remarked, "It will be late when we get there. You must stay with my family and then go to synagogue with us on the Sabbath." Sha'uwl (Paul) replied, "Your kind gesture is accepted." The next morning, they began their trip and after two days reached their set destination but when.....

"Unseen Footsteps of Jesus"
OLAM
HABA
(Future World)
Mysteries Book 1- "Pre Dawn"
Jerry Ayers

"Unseen Footsteps of Jesus"
OLAM
HABA
(Future World)
Mysteries Book 2- "The Dawning"
Jerry Ayers

"Unseen Footsteps of Jesus"
OLAM
HABA
(Future World)
Jerry Ayers

"Unseen Footsteps of Jesus"
OLAM
HABA
(Future World)
Mysteries Book 4- "The Rising Sun"
Jerry Ayers

"Unseen Footsteps of Jesus"
OLAM
HABA
(Future World)
Mysteries Book 5- "Storm Clouds"
Jerry Ayers

"Unseen Footsteps of Jesus"
OLAM
HABA
(Future World)
Jerry Ayers

"Unseen Footsteps of Jesus"
OLAM
HABA
(Future World)
Jerry Ayers

OLAM
HABA
(Future World)
Jerry Ayers